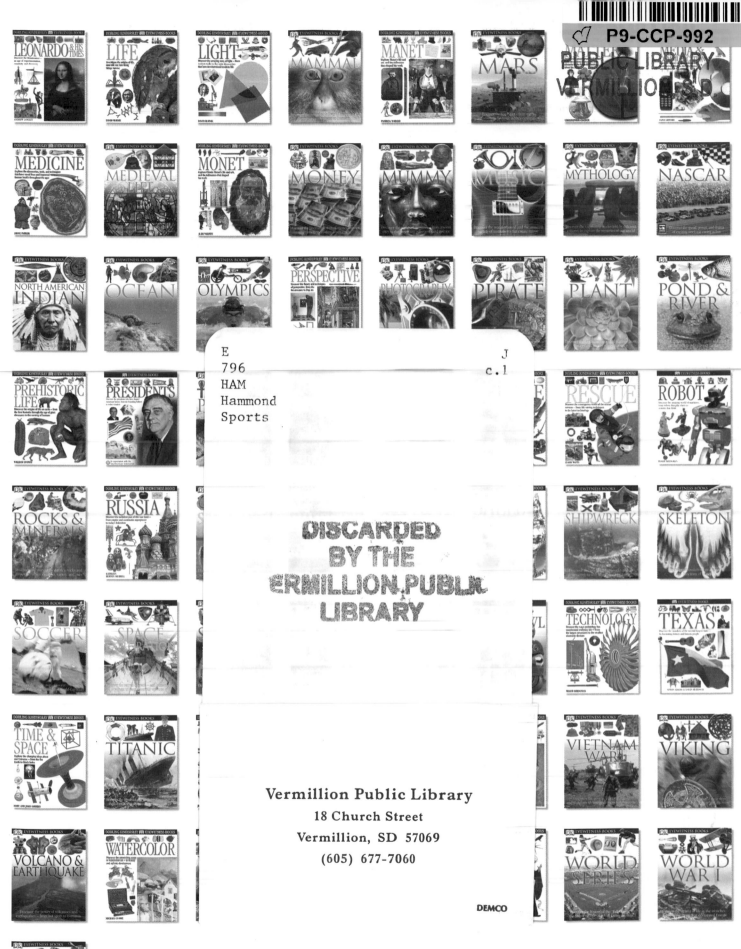

Eyewitness
SPORTS

Badminton racket

Golf club

Boxing glove

Golf ball

Baseball glove
and ball

Javelin

Dumbbell

Arrows

Eyewitness
SPORTS

Starting pistol

Written by
TIM HAMMOND

Cricket batting glove

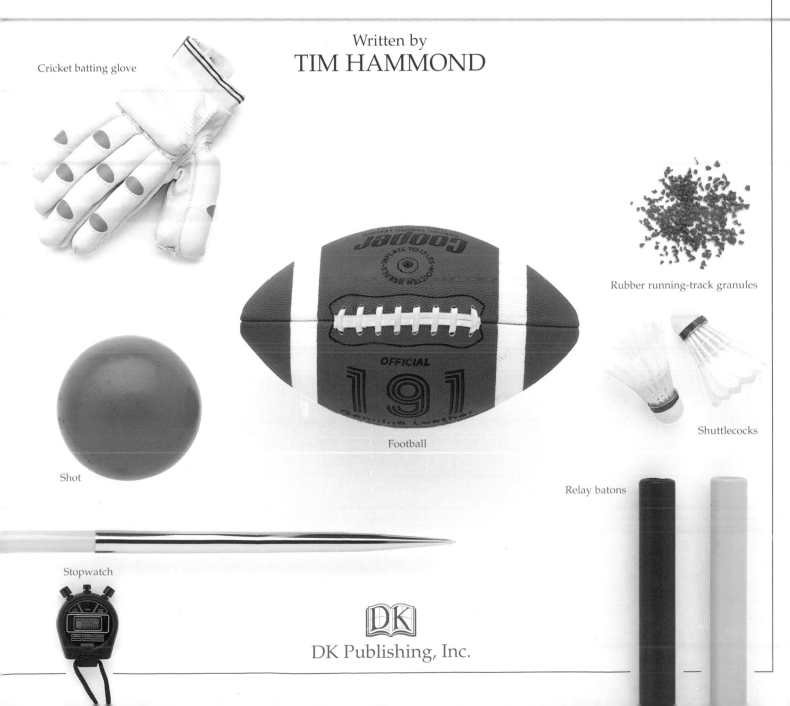

Rubber running-track granules

Shuttlecocks

Football

Shot

Relay batons

Stopwatch

DK
DK Publishing, Inc.

Tennis ball

Shuttlecock

Referee's
whistle

Hockey stick

DK

LONDON, NEW YORK, MUNICH,
MELBOURNE, and DELHI

Project editor Tim Hammond
Art editor Mike Clowes
Managing editor Vicky Davenport
Managing art editor Jane Owen
Special photography Dave King
Editorial consultants
The staff of the Natural History Museum London

REVISED EDITION
Editors Barbara Berger, Laura Buller
Editorial assistant John Searcy
Publishing director Beth Sutinis
Senior designer Tai Blanche
Designers Jessica Lasher, Diana Catherines
Photo research Chrissy McIntyre
Art director Dirk Kaufman
DTP designer Milos Orlovic
Production Ivor Parker

Dart

This Eyewitness ® Guide has been conceived by
Dorling Kindersley Limited and Editions Gallimard

This edition published in the United States in 2005
by DK Publishing, Inc.
375 Hudson Street, New York, NY 10014

05 06 07 08 09 10 9 8 7 6 5 4 3 2 1

Pool balls

Golf tees

Measuring tape

A catalog record for this book is
available from the Library of Congress.

ISBN 0-7566-1390-6 (Hardcover) 0-7566-1399-X (Library Binding)

Color reproduction by Colourscan, Singapore
Printed in China by Toppan Printing Co.,
(Shenzhen) Ltd.

Squash ball

Discover more at
www.dk.com

Headband

Spiked
track shoe

Contents

Soccer shoe studs

Cricket ball

Soccer

SOCCER IS A TEAM SPORT in which players attempt to score goals by kicking or "heading" a ball into the opposing team's goal. Except for the goalkeeper, the players are not allowed to intentionally touch the ball with their hands or arms, unless they are throwing it in from the sideline. Games in which a ball is kicked have been played around the world in various forms for centuries: soldiers in ancient China played "football" as part of their army training - using the head of an enemy warrior as the ball! In 15th-century England, the sport was banned by the king because men preferred it to practicing their archery, and many were so badly injured in the violent matches that they could not fight in the army. Soccer is one of a group of sports - including football and rugby - that grew out of these early "games." It is the most popular sport in the world and is played and enjoyed by millions.

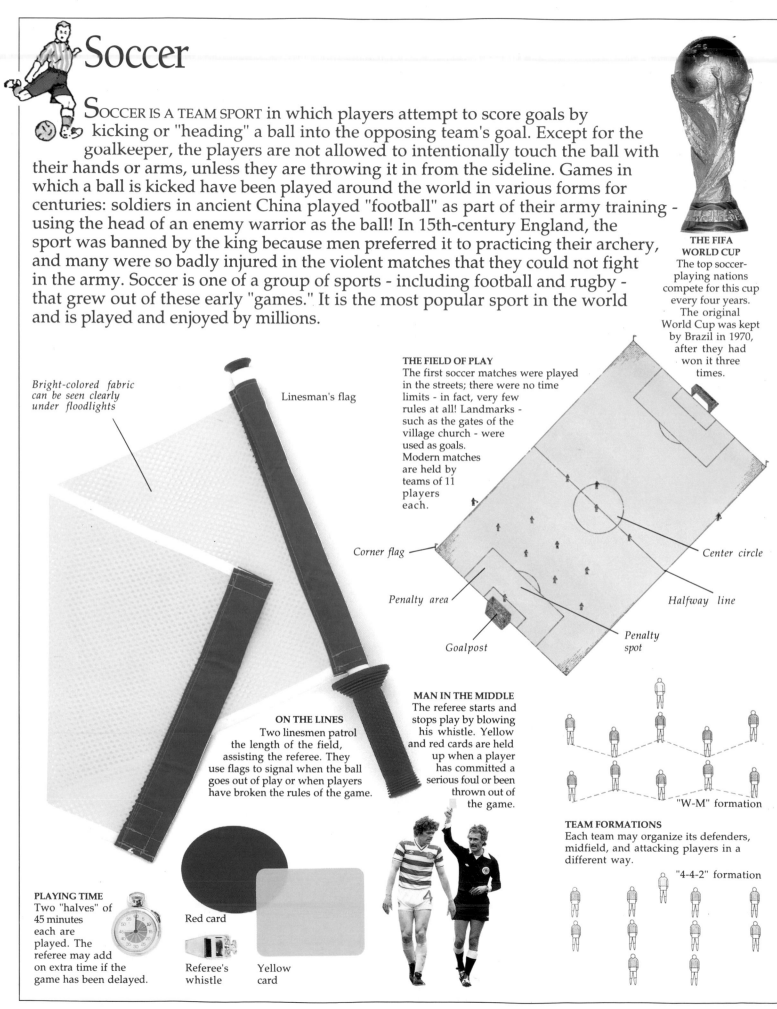

THE FIFA WORLD CUP
The top soccer-playing nations compete for this cup every four years. The original World Cup was kept by Brazil in 1970, after they had won it three times.

Bright-colored fabric can be seen clearly under floodlights

Linesman's flag

THE FIELD OF PLAY
The first soccer matches were played in the streets; there were no time limits - in fact, very few rules at all! Landmarks - such as the gates of the village church - were used as goals. Modern matches are held by teams of 11 players each.

Corner flag

Center circle

Penalty area

Halfway line

Goalpost

Penalty spot

ON THE LINES
Two linesmen patrol the length of the field, assisting the referee. They use flags to signal when the ball goes out of play or when players have broken the rules of the game.

MAN IN THE MIDDLE
The referee starts and stops play by blowing his whistle. Yellow and red cards are held up when a player has committed a serious foul or been thrown out of the game.

"W-M" formation

TEAM FORMATIONS
Each team may organize its defenders, midfield, and attacking players in a different way.

"4-4-2" formation

PLAYING TIME
Two "halves" of 45 minutes each are played. The referee may add on extra time if the game has been delayed.

Red card

Referee's whistle

Yellow card

6

Soccer fashions

The modern soccer player's clothing has changed greatly from that worn by the first professionals over a hundred years ago. For example, players did not wear numbers on their shirts. Instead, the uniform of each player was different from that of his teammates, so he could only be identified by the color of his cap or his socks! Perhaps the most noticeable change has been in footwear: the clumsy "armored" shoes of the last century have changed gradually into the flexible and sophisticated modern shoes that are now only a third as heavy.

1880s *above*
At this time it was normal to kick the ball with the toe, so shoes were made with steel or chrome toecaps to protect the kicker's feet. Pads were worn outside the socks to protect shins against stray kicks!

Leather sole

Mid 20th-century shoes

1930s-1950s
Despite the baggy shorts, the player's uniform was now lighter, but the shoes still weighed around 1 lb (500 g) each.

More streamlined shape

Arthur Rowe Sleekline

Shoes reached above the ankle

Early 20th-century shoes

Leather studs tacked on to sole

THE GOALKEEPER
The goalkeeper is the only player allowed to handle the ball. His shirt is a different color from the other players'. Many goalkeepers also wear gloves to help them grip the ball, and peaked caps to shade their eyes from the sun.

ARTIFICIAL GRASS
Grass fields get very wet and boggy during the winter, so some teams play on fields made from synthetic materials that are unaffected by the weather. However, artificial fields are more common in football (p. 10).

1980s *below*
Modern soccer shoes weigh only about 8 oz (250 g) or less. The development of such light and flexible shoes went hand-in-hand with changing playing styles; as footballers became more skillful, they needed shoes that allowed them to have better speed and ball control.

Late 20th-century shoes

Rubber studs *Aluminum studs* *Nylon studs*

INTERCHANGEABLE STUDS
Studs of different materials and sizes are suitable for different field conditions - flat rubber studs for hard ground, aluminum for wet and slippery conditions, and nylon when the field is soft but firm.

"ASTRO SHOES"
Soccer shoes with interchangeable studs are unsuitable for Astroturf and other artificial fields. Instead, modified training shoes are usually worn. A pattern of tiny molded studs or "pimples" provides the most comfortable shoe and the best grip. This shoe has 73 more "studs" than a normal soccer shoe!

How soccer balls are made

Nowadays soccer balls - as well as the balls used in some other sports - are often made from synthetic materials molded into the correct shape. However, the balls used by professional teams have always been made from leather panels stitched together around a rubber bladder, and the best balls are still made this way. Leather balls have better air resistance, so they don't wobble in flight.

Untreated leather scuffed easily

Final seam had to be laced up

ROUGH AND TUMBLE
The early soccer matches were rowdy affairs, with teams of 100 or more charging through the streets chasing a ball made from an inflated pig's bladder.

Soccer in the Middle Ages

PRE-WAR BALL
Until the 1940s footballs were always tan colored. They were not as waterproof as modern balls, so they became very heavy in wet conditions. The technique for stitching up the final panels of the ball had not yet been invented, so these balls were always laced.

Making a leather ball

Holes punched in panels for stitching

One needle is used at each end of the waxed thread

Maker's name stamped onto panels

Edges cut to fit together perfectly

1 CUTTING THE PANELS
The leather is coated in special paint to make it waterproof, and a strong lining is stuck to the back to make the leather stiffer and keep it from stretching. The firmest leather is used to make the most expensive balls; softer leather stretches more easily and is used for cheaper, practice balls. Two types of panel are cut out, using special knives. There are 18 panels in this type of ball.

Threads twisted together and rubbed with wax

2 STITCHING THE PANELS TOGETHER
Now the stitcher begins to join the leather panels together, using two needles and a special waxed thread made up of five strands. The wax makes the thread waterproof and easier to use. The panels are held together in a special clamp (*see opposite*) gripped between the stitcher's knees so he can have both hands free.

Old-fashioned ball-making tools

THE STITCHING HORSE
The ball maker sits on a special bench that has a clamp that holds the leather panels tightly while he stitches them together.

These panels are for a rugby ball, (p. 14), which is made in a similar way to a soccer ball

Clamp gripped between knees

Clamp secured by adjustable metal grip

32-PANEL BALL
Balls can be made in several different ways. The main difference is in the number and shape of the panels. This ball is made with a combination of 12 five-sided and 20 six-sided panels.

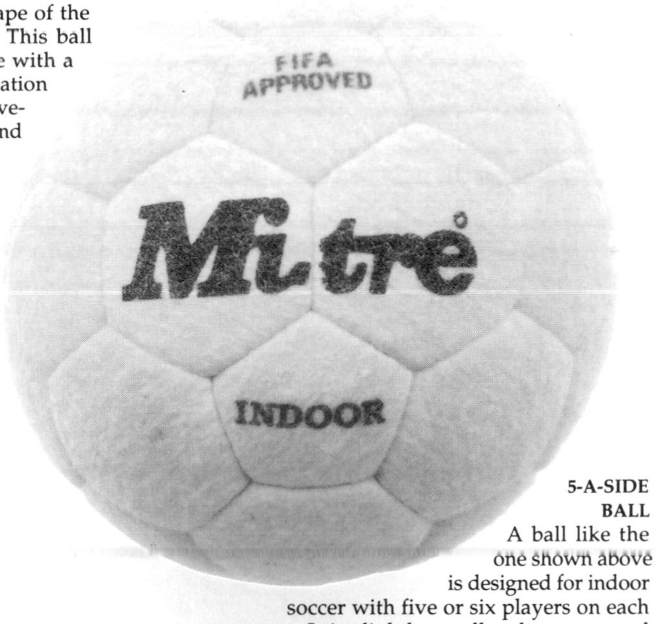

FIFA APPROVED

Mitre

INDOOR

5-A-SIDE BALL
A ball like the one shown above is designed for indoor soccer with five or six players on each team. It is slightly smaller than a normal soccer ball and made from soft, feltlike material that has a low bounce ideal for indoor games.

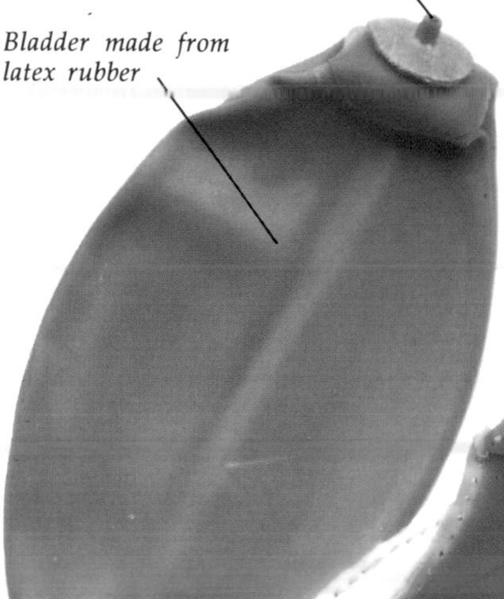

Bladder valve

Bladder made from latex rubber

ALTERNATIVE DESIGN
The players in this 1924 match are using a ball made from just 12 panels - the fewer panels there are, the less perfectly round the ball will be.

Finished ball weighs 14-16 oz (400-500 g)

5

MINERVA SUPREME

GUARANTEED HAND SEWN

THE MINERVA® FOOTBALL CO. LTD.

FIFA APPROVED

ENGLAND

Panels sewn together with ball inside out

The ball will be kicked and headed thousands of times throughout its life

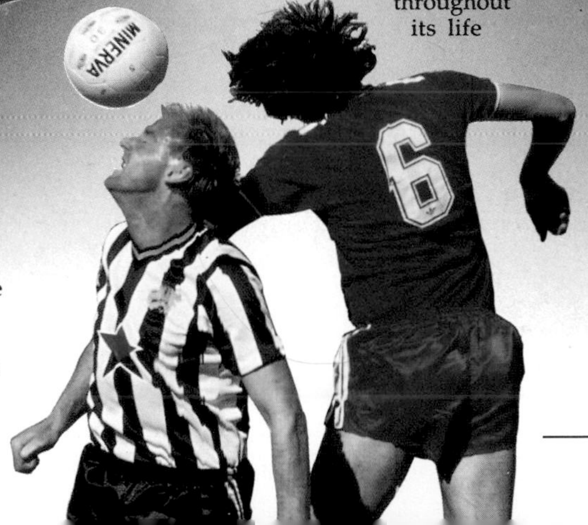

3 FORMING THE SHAPE OF THE BALL
The seams on each set of three panels are hammered flat to make the ball as round as possible. With the ball inside out, the panels are then sewn together at right angles to each other. The seams are hammered again to make sure the corners are smooth, and the ball is turned the right way around. The last side of the ball is partly sewn on, leaving enough room for the stitcher to push the rubber bladder into the ball. The air valve of the bladder fits through a hole punched into one of the panels.

4 THE FINISHED BALL
With the ball the right way out, the stitcher begins the difficult task of sewing up the final seam. He cannot tie off the thread in a knot or it would show on the outside of the ball, so he sews it back into the ball and cuts off the ends as close as he can. The ball is given a thorough inspection to check for any faults and is blown up with air to the correct pressure. Each ball takes about three and a half hours to make.

Football

Padded-up
football player
in full flight

FOOTBALL IS AN EXCITING SPORT played by two teams of 11 players each; with separate squads for defense and offense, up to 40 men can play for a team during a single game. The tactics can be very complicated, but the object is simple - to score points by crossing the opponents' goal line with the ball (a touchdown) or by kicking the ball between their goalposts. The game is therefore based on each team's attempt to advance up the field toward the other's goal. It was first played in American colleges in the late 19th century and is, without doubt, the team sport with the greatest amount of physical contact. The helmets and huge shoulder pads worn by the players help make this one of the most spectacular of all sports to watch. Canadian football has slightly different rules.

Football helmet

Face mask
made from
unbreakable
plastic coated
in rubber

SHOCK ABSORBERS *below*
Inside the helmet,
cells filled with air
or antifreeze liquid
help prevent injury by
spreading impact evenly.

Goal line

Hashmarks
every yard

Goalpost

End zone

THE GRIDIRON
Each team can make four attempts to advance 10 yd (9 m) up the field; each attempt is called a "down." If they succeed, they play another four downs; otherwise their opponents win possession of the ball. The gridiron (field) is marked out in yards to show how far a team has advanced.

Numbers every 10 yards
with arrows pointing
to nearest goal line

Yard lines
every 5 yards

HEAD CASES
Every player must wear a proper helmet with a protective face mask. The first "helmets" were made from boiled leather. The modern ones are tough plastic. Most players also use a mouthpiece to protect their teeth.

MODERN WARRIORS
"War paint" was first worn by the Washington Redskins. The players found that painting their cheeks this way helped reduce glare from the sun. Other teams did the same, and face paint is now a common sight.

...AND THE ORIGINAL
The names of many football teams reflect the aggressive nature of the sport. Each game is like a battle, with teams advancing and retreating.

Cincinnati Bengals

Los Angeles Rams

Philadelphia Eagles

New York Jets

San Diego Chargers

Buffalo Bills

Seattle Seahawks

New York Giants

NFL HELMETS
The names of the 28 teams in the National Football League (NFL) are made up of their city name and a nickname. The helmets worn by the teams often bear a logo relating to their nicknames.

Shoulder pads

BROAD SHOULDERS
Shoulder and chest pads can weigh up to 5.5 lb (2.5 kg), depending on the position of the player.

Upper arm pads can be attached to shoulder pads

TACKLE DUMMY
Players build strength and practice their blocking technique on this special piece of equipment.

ARM PADS
The amount of padding worn by each player depends on how fast and agile he must be to do his particular job.

Fingerless gloves give protection and freedom of movement

BIKE®

Elbow pad

GLOVES
Some players wear gloves to protect their hands and help them grip the ball; others use adhesive tape.

FOOTBALL SHIRTS
Some players wear tight-fitting shirts that are difficult for opponents to grab. Others wear shirts made of flimsy fabric that simply tears away if pulled. The numbers on the front must be at least 8 in (20 cm) high, and those on the back at least 10 in (25 cm).

WHAT NUMBER?
Each team is made up of three groups: offense, defense, and special units for kicking. There are no strict rules about numbers, but number 34 is often worn by a running back.

11

The need for padding

Early forms of football were very dangerous - in 1905, for example, 18 college players were killed and over 150 badly injured. This led to changes in the rules about protective clothing to help make the sport safer. Many players use adhesive tape as a form of protection - some professional teams can use over 300 miles of tape in a season!

RIB PADS *left*
Apart from their helmets and bulky shoulder pads, players wear padding to prevent injuries to the lower parts of their body. The rib pads are like a corset with a hard plastic shell; they tie on to the shoulder pads and lace up at the front.

Straps tie on to shoulder pads

HIP AND GROIN PADS *below*
The protection for the hip area is made up of three separate pads - one for each hip and one for the groin. These are held together by straps that are threaded through each pad and done up at the back.

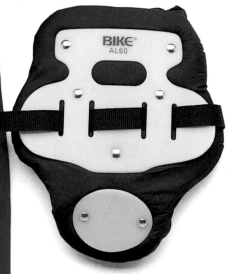

Rigid plastic covering

Foam-sponge filling

Thigh pads

Leg pads slipped under tight-fitting pants

Knee pads

PANTS *above*
The padding for the hips and legs is worn underneath close-fitting knee-length pants that lace up at the front.

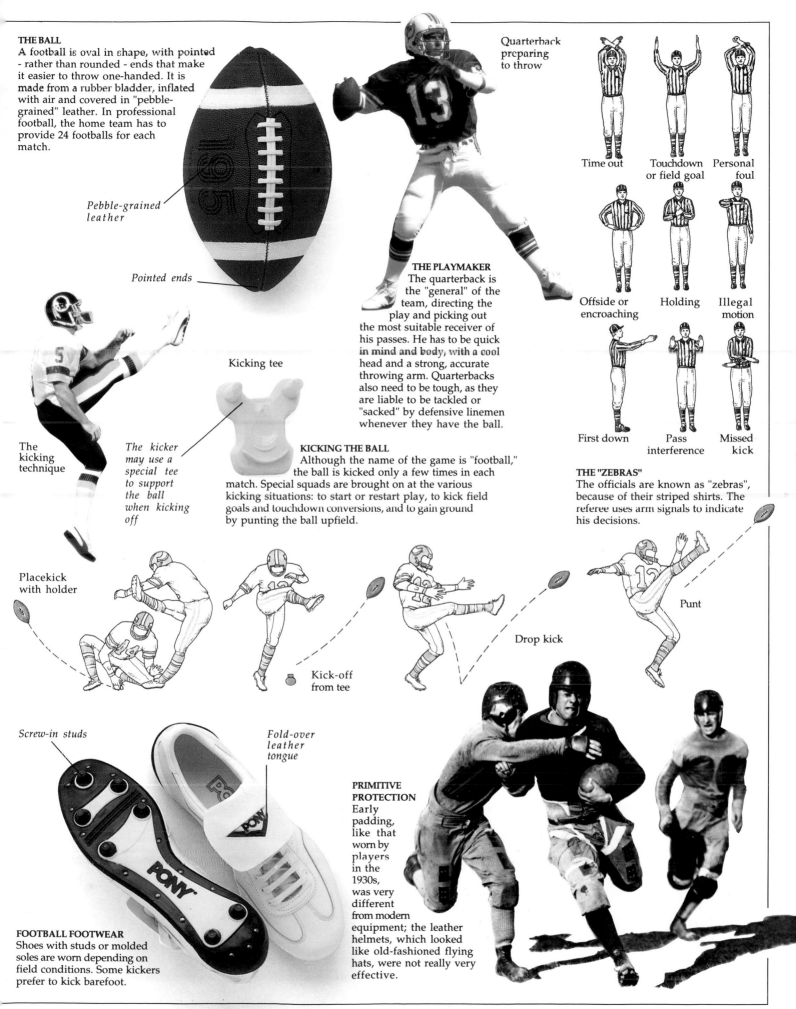

THE BALL
A football is oval in shape, with pointed - rather than rounded - ends that make it easier to throw one-handed. It is made from a rubber bladder, inflated with air and covered in "pebble-grained" leather. In professional football, the home team has to provide 24 footballs for each match.

Pebble-grained leather

Pointed ends

Quarterback preparing to throw

Time out

Touchdown or field goal

Personal foul

Offside or encroaching

Holding

Illegal motion

First down

Pass interference

Missed kick

THE PLAYMAKER
The quarterback is the "general" of the team, directing the play and picking out the most suitable receiver of his passes. He has to be quick in mind and body, with a cool head and a strong, accurate throwing arm. Quarterbacks also need to be tough, as they are liable to be tackled or "sacked" by defensive linemen whenever they have the ball.

The kicking technique

Kicking tee

The kicker may use a special tee to support the ball when kicking off

KICKING THE BALL
Although the name of the game is "football," the ball is kicked only a few times in each match. Special squads are brought on at the various kicking situations: to start or restart play, to kick field goals and touchdown conversions, and to gain ground by punting the ball upfield.

THE "ZEBRAS"
The officials are known as "zebras", because of their striped shirts. The referee uses arm signals to indicate his decisions.

Placekick with holder

Kick-off from tee

Drop kick

Punt

Screw-in studs

Fold-over leather tongue

FOOTBALL FOOTWEAR
Shoes with studs or molded soles are worn depending on field conditions. Some kickers prefer to kick barefoot.

PRIMITIVE PROTECTION
Early padding, like that worn by players in the 1930s, was very different from modern equipment; the leather helmets, which looked like old-fashioned flying hats, were not really very effective.

Rugby

RUGBY IS A SPORT in which players are allowed to carry, kick, and throw the ball (but they can only throw it backward). Points are scored by touching the ball down over the opponents' goal line (a "try") or by kicking it over the crossbar and between the goalposts. The sport gets its name from Rugby high school in England where it was first played in 1823. The "inventor" of the sport was William Webb Ellis, a pupil at the school, who was the first player to pick up and run with the ball during a soccer game. In 1895 an argument over paying money to players led to a split between rugby clubs in England. Two forms of the sport have existed ever since: the newer, professional (paid) game is known as Rugby League, and has thirteen players per team. The more traditional and widely-played amateur (unpaid) version is Rugby Union, with fifteen players on each side. The rules for each are slightly different, but the basic idea behind both sports remains the same.

Scoring a try

THE WEBB ELLIS CUP
This trophy, named after the founder of the sport, was first competed for in 1987. The winner was New Zealand, which beat France in the final.

TRADITIONAL QUALITY
The company that makes these international match balls was supplying soccer balls to Rugby high school in 1823, when the game was first played there.

Modern leather rugby ball

HUMAN SPIDER
When the teams lock together into a "scrum" (face-off), they look like a giant spider with many legs. The players in the middle of the scrum are the "hookers," who try to heel the ball backward for their team-mates to pick up.

SKY-SCRAPERS AND SIDE-WINDERS *below*
The tallest Rugby Union goalposts in the world are 110 ft (33.5 m) high. Most players today kick the ball soccer-style rather than with the toe of the shoe and are known as "side-winders" because of their curved run-up and kicking action.

High-sided rugby shoe

BOOTING THE BALL *left*
Rugby players may wear soccer shoes or special, high-sided shoes that support the ankles. The longest recorded goal kick was scored in 1932, when the ball was kicked 270 ft (82 m).

MAORI WARDANCE
The New Zealand national team is known as the All Blacks because of its all-black uniform. The first New Zealand touring team consisted mainly of native Maori players who performed a traditional wardance called a "haka" before each game. This is still a feature of matches played by the modern All Blacks.

AWARDING CAPS
The practice of giving special caps was introduced at Rugby high school as a way of thanking team members for their efforts. Caps are now awarded in other sports too, when players are chosen to play for their country.

1908 Rugby cap

Rounder-style ball made in 1851

THE EVOLUTION OF THE BALL *left*
Early rugby balls were much rounder than they are today. The modern shape makes the ball much easier to carry and throw.

RUNNING WITH THE BALL
One of the most exciting plays in a rugby match is when a player catches the ball and runs the whole length of the field to score a try - hotly pursued by opposing players.

Rugby balls are made from four leather panels, stitched together in the same way as soccer balls (p. 8)

ALTERNATIVE MATERIALS *right*
Over the years, ball makers have tried making balls out of various materials besides the traditional leather. Pig skin, and even camel skin, are excellent materials to work with, but balls made from them were found to be too slippery.

Camel skin ball

Field hockey

FIELD HOCKEY HAS BEEN DESCRIBED in a very simple way as "soccer played with a stick and a cricket ball in place of a soccer ball" and there are, indeed, many ways in which the two sports are alike. Field hockey is played by teams of 11 men or women, and no physical contact is allowed. Ancient Egyptian and Greek wall paintings suggest that games like field hockey were played as far back as the third century B.C., and the Romans are known to have played a game called *paganica*, which used curved sticks and a leather-covered ball. The modern sport is based on the *hurling*, *bandy*, and *shinty* games played in different areas of the British Isles, although the name "hockey" is thought to come from the French word *hoquet*, meaning a "hooked stick."

VICTORIAN PLAYER
Field hockey as it is played today first became popular in England in the late 19th century.

THE GOALKEEPER
The goalie wears extra padding, including a chest protector and a helmet with a face mask, to protect him from shots hit at up to 100 mph (160 kmh).

Goalkeeper's helmet

Striking circle

25 yd (22 m) line

THE MODERN GAME *left*
Hockey is played indoors and outdoors, at all levels from school- to Olympic-standard, by men and women, and on grass or synthetic fields.

THE FIELD
Goals can only be scored from inside the opposing team's striking circle. The goals themselves are small - just 12 ft (3.6 m) wide and 7 ft (2.1 m) high .

Halfway line

Penalty spot

Outdoor stick

TRIBAL GAMES *below*
The earliest form of lacrosse was called *baggataway* and was played by North American Indians as part of their training for war.

Lacrosse ball

Nets made from gut, rawhide, or cord

Plastic net frame

KICKERS
The goalkeeper is the only player allowed to intentionally touch the ball with his feet. He wears special "kickers" outside his shoes, with which he blocks the ball and kicks it clear of his goal.

Rigid palm 2 in (5 cm) thick

Straps fit over normal shoes

Padded toes protect feet against the hard ball

FOOTWEAR
The shoes worn by field hockey players depend on the surface they are playing on. Soccer-style shoes are usually worn on grass, and special multi-studded shoes like these on synthetic fields.

GAUNTLETS
The goalie's gloves are different for each hand. One is flexible, so he can pick the ball up when he has to, and the other has a rigid, padded palm that is used to stop the ball.

Padding extends below the wrist to protect the forearm

Over 60 molded studs on each sole

STICK HEADS *below*
Sticks have a rounded side and a flat face, with which the ball is struck. No part of the stick is allowed to be more than 2 in (5 cm) wide.

Indoor stick

THE BALL
The hard hockey ball is similar in size to a baseball or cricket ball and is usually white.

TYPES OF STICKS *above*
Most modern sticks are made from ash, with a cane handle. The head is steam-bent so that the grain of the wood follows the bend and strengthens the stick. Indoor sticks are lighter and thinner; old-fashioned sticks had a longer curve.

A woman player of 1912

Old-fashioned stick

Lacrosse

This sport is similar to field hockey but uses sticks with nets to throw, catch, and carry the ball. French settlers in North America gave the sport its name - the hooked sticks reminded them of a bishop's staff or *crozier* ("la crosse"). Men's and women's games are played differently.

Women's lacrosse sticks are generally shorter than men's

LACROSSE STICK
Sticks are traditionally made from hickory wood, but many are now made from plastic. The net must be tightly strung so the ball does not become stuck.

INDIAN CROSSE *right*
The type of stick used by the first players varied according to which tribe they came from. Many were decorated with feathers.

Ice hockey

As its name suggests, ice hockey is basically hockey played on ice, and it originated as the winter version of field hockey - played on frozen ponds and lakes. However, there are several other major differences between the modern forms of the two sports: Ice hockey teams have six players who use longer sticks and a hard rubber disk, called a puck, instead of a ball. Modern ice hockey is usually played indoors, where the temperature of the ice is controlled automatically. The ice is cleaned off between each of the three 20-minute periods.

Ice hockey helmet

A modern player in full uniform

SPEEDY SPORT
Ice hockey is the fastest team sport in the world. There is also a great deal of body contact, and the players wear padding to protect them when they crash into the barriers that surround the rink.

Elbow pad

BODY ARMOR
As well as the items shown here, ice hockey players wear special shorts that have thick padding sewn into them to protect the players' legs when they fall on the hard ice. Deliberately tripping an opponent is against the rules, and the offender would be punished by spending time in the penalty box. Depending on how bad the offense was, the penalty lasts from two to ten minutes.

Shoulder and chest padding

GLOVES
The gauntlets worn by skaters players are heavily padded and made from leather or synthetic materials. Rigid fingertip caps provide extra protection. Goalkeepers wear a different kind of glove on each hand - a "catcher" and a "blocker."

FROZEN PUCK
The disk-shaped puck is made from vulcanized (toughened) rubber. It is generally kept frozen before a match so that it keeps its original form as long as possible.

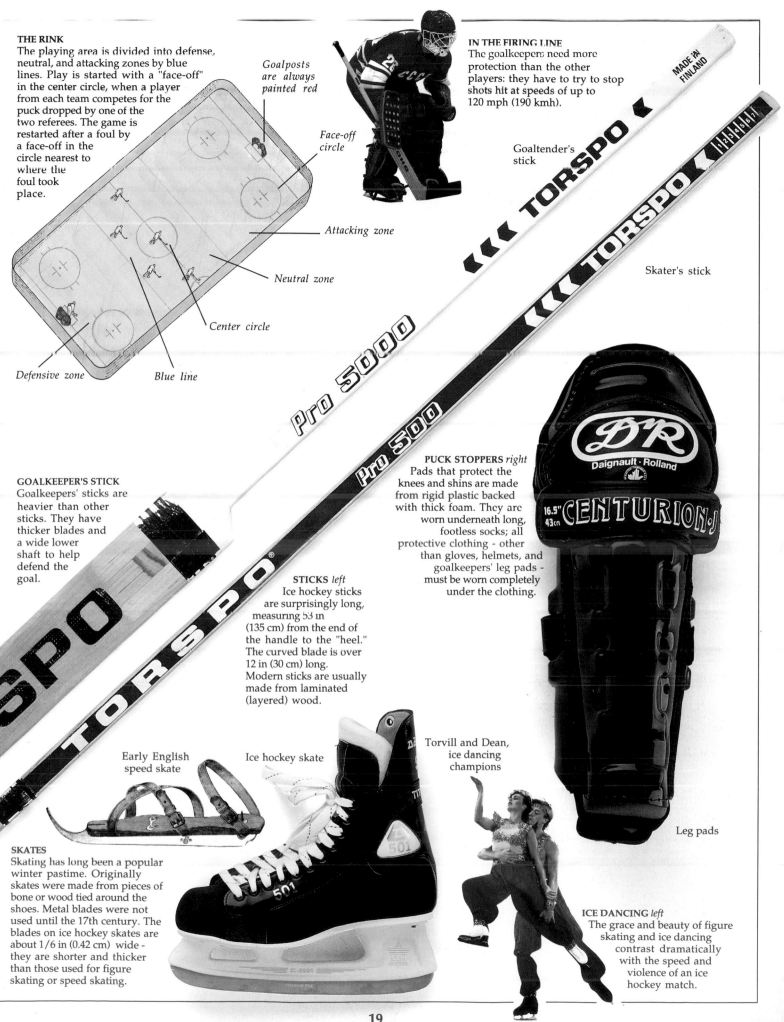

THE RINK
The playing area is divided into defense, neutral, and attacking zones by blue lines. Play is started with a "face-off" in the center circle, when a player from each team competes for the puck dropped by one of the two referees. The game is restarted after a foul by a face-off in the circle nearest to where the foul took place.

Goalposts are always painted red

Face-off circle

Attacking zone

Neutral zone

Center circle

Defensive zone

Blue line

IN THE FIRING LINE
The goalkeepers need more protection than the other players: they have to try to stop shots hit at speeds of up to 120 mph (190 kmh).

Goaltender's stick

Skater's stick

GOALKEEPER'S STICK
Goalkeepers' sticks are heavier than other sticks. They have thicker blades and a wide lower shaft to help defend the goal.

PUCK STOPPERS *right*
Pads that protect the knees and shins are made from rigid plastic backed with thick foam. They are worn underneath long, footless socks; all protective clothing - other than gloves, helmets, and goalkeepers' leg pads - must be worn completely under the clothing.

STICKS *left*
Ice hockey sticks are surprisingly long, measuring 53 in (135 cm) from the end of the handle to the "heel." The curved blade is over 12 in (30 cm) long. Modern sticks are usually made from laminated (layered) wood.

Early English speed skate

Ice hockey skate

Torvill and Dean, ice dancing champions

Leg pads

SKATES
Skating has long been a popular winter pastime. Originally skates were made from pieces of bone or wood tied around the shoes. Metal blades were not used until the 17th century. The blades on ice hockey skates are about 1/6 in (0.42 cm) wide - they are shorter and thicker than those used for figure skating or speed skating.

ICE DANCING *left*
The grace and beauty of figure skating and ice dancing contrast dramatically with the speed and violence of an ice hockey match.

Basketball

IN 1891, A CLERGYMAN in America invented the game of basketball when he nailed a peach basket to the balcony at each end of the local gymnasium. The object of the game is to score points by throwing the ball into the "basket" at your opponents' end of the court. Basketball is a nonviolent sport, played indoors, in which the five players on each team throw and bounce the ball, but cannot carry or kick it. Because of the height of the baskets, there are many very tall basketball players - the tallest being 8ft (2.45 m)!

Harlem Globetrotter

The basketball has a circumference of 30-31 in (75-78 cm)

Basketball hoop

TIME-OUT
Both teams can call a one-minute time-out twice in each half of the match to discuss tactics.

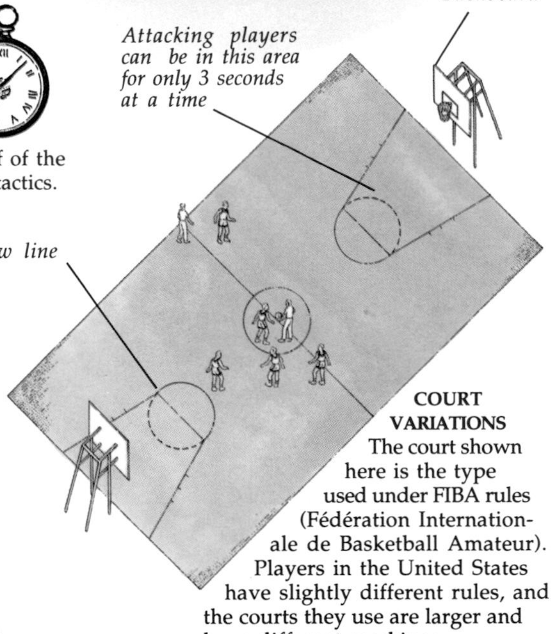

Backboard

Attacking players can be in this area for only 3 seconds at a time

Free-throw line

COURT VARIATIONS
The court shown here is the type used under FIBA rules (Fédération Internationale de Basketball Amateur). Players in the United States have slightly different rules, and the courts they use are larger and have different markings.

Player making a dunk-shot

Basketball shoes have high, padded ankles for added support.

CONVERSE®

Netball

Netball is played almost entirely by women. It is similar to basketball but played on a slightly larger court, with seven players on each side rather than five, and nets supported by poles instead of backboards. Like basketball, it originated in the United States in the second half of the last century.

MOVING WITH THE BALL
Netball players are not allowed to carry the ball. When holding it, the player can turn in any direction, but must keep one of her feet on the same spot.

Netball

PLAYING ZONES
Each player is only allowed in certain areas of the court. Players wear lettered vests to indicate their positions so the umpire knows if a player is in the wrong zone.

Volleyball

This sport is like a cross between basketball and badminton (p. 35). Teams of six players hit a ball over a net using their hands and arms or any other part of their upper body. Each team may touch the ball up to three times before it crosses the net.

AT THE NET *left*
The height of the net means that attacking players have to jump high to smash the ball downward. No player is allowed to touch the net or reach over it into the opposing team's side of the court.

THE BALL *right*
The volleyball is lightweight and of a uniform color. It is smaller than a netball or a basketball.

Baseball

THE OFFICIAL NATIONAL SPORT of the United States, baseball is very similar to a number of earlier bat-and-ball games such as the English game "rounders," which was introduced by the early settlers in the 18th century. The game is divided into nine periods called innings, with each team of nine players batting and the other team fielding. The batters have to hit the ball and run between fixed bases to score runs for their team; the fielders try to put the batters out in different ways - including catching the ball before it bounces and tagging a runner with the ball as he runs between bases. Some of the stars of the sport are those who can hit the ball the farthest, the record being more than 618 ft (188 m).

Joe DiMaggio, c. 1940s

THE HOMER
If a batter hits the ball far enough in fair territory, he can run around all four bases at once, scoring a home run. The shortest time taken to run around the bases - a distance of some 360 ft (108 m) - is 13.3 seconds.

HANDY HEADGEAR
Players have been seriously injured and even killed by baseballs pitched at speeds of up to 100 mph (160 kmh), so the plastic helmet worn by the batter is a very necessary piece of equipment.

Batter's helmet

The left-handed Babe Ruth, c. 1920s

The strike zone

Wooden bat

Aluminum bat

THE STRIKE ZONE
This is the area directly above home plate and between the batter's armpits and his knees. Any ball pitched in this area is called as a strike. The batter has up to three strikes to try and hit the ball into fair territory.

BATS
Only wooden bats are allowed in the top-class major league baseball, although aluminum ones last longer and hit the ball farther. The barrel of the bat must be perfectly round.

GLOVES
Most batters wear one or two thin leather gloves to keep blisters from forming on their hands.

SHIRTS

Shirts cannot have any pattern or emblem that could be mistaken for a baseball, or any shiny glass or polished metal that could reflect the sun into another player's eyes. Each shirt must have a number at least 6 in (15 cm) high on the back. Some players also wear long-sleeved undershirts.

Baseball

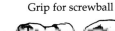

INSIDE THE BALL

The baseball weighs between 5 and 5.5 oz (142-156 g), and has a very complex structure. Top-quality balls are covered in cowhide or horsehide treated with alum and are handstitched.

Red outer stitching

PITCHING

The pitcher must be able to throw fast and slow balls that curve in the air in various directions. The way the ball is gripped partly determines the type of pitch delivered.

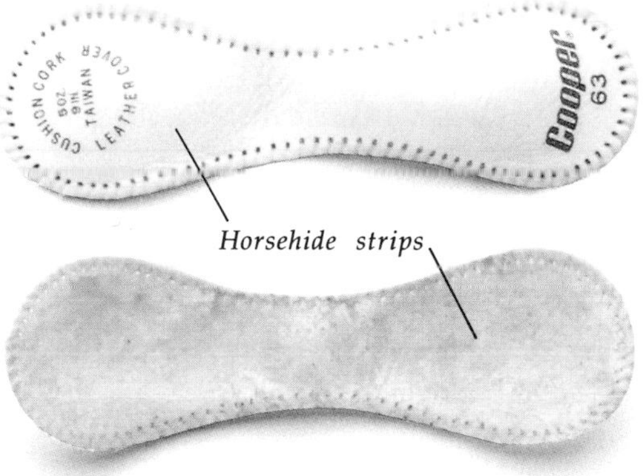

Grip for screwball

Horsehide strips

Woolen strands

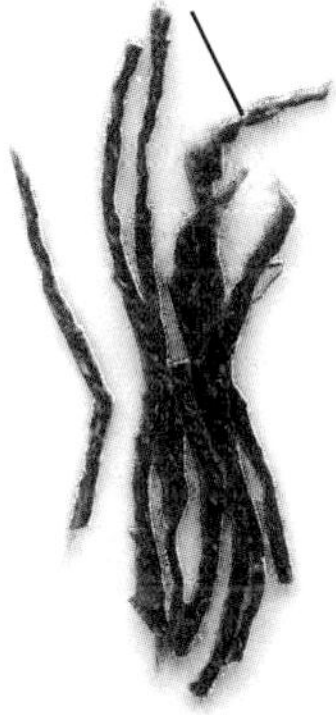

Cork center

Woolen yarn

Rubber inner casing

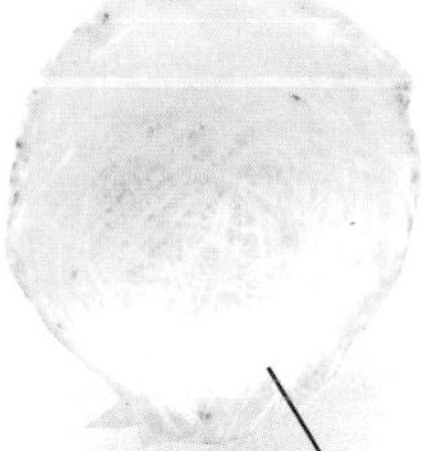

Cotton thread outer casing

A baseball pitcher

AN INTERNATIONAL SPORT

Although baseball is primarily an American sport, it is played by enthusiasts in other countries too. The International Baseball Association is the coordinating body of the sport around the world.

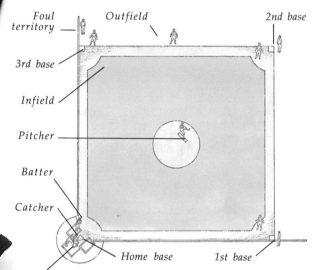

Foul territory · Outfield · 2nd base · 3rd base · Infield · Pitcher · Batter · Catcher · Home base · 1st base · Umpire

THE DIAMOND

The baseball diamond is bordered by the four base paths that surround the infield. The area outside this is divided into the outfield and foul territory - into which the ball should not be hit. The home plate and the pitcher's rubber are slabs of white rubber, and the other bases are made from canvas bags filled with soft material.

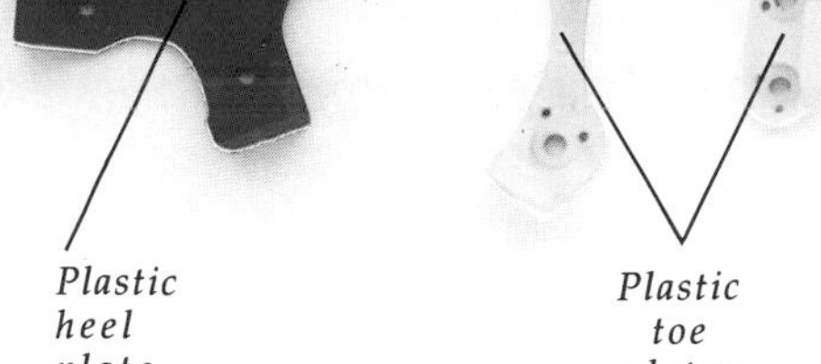

Baseball pants

PANTS

The traditional baseball outfit includes pants that reach just below the knee. Separate stirrups are worn over the socks.

Stirrups

SLIDING INTO BASE

A batter is forced out if a player with the ball touches first base before he does. At other bases, runners will dive head-first into the base to avoid getting tagged out.

Metal shoe plates

Plastic heel plate

Plastic toe plates

BASEBALL SHOES

As with other sports, the type of shoes worn depends on whether the surface is natural or synthetic grass. Toe and heel plates are screwed to the sole of shoes worn on natural grass; pointed spikes are not allowed.

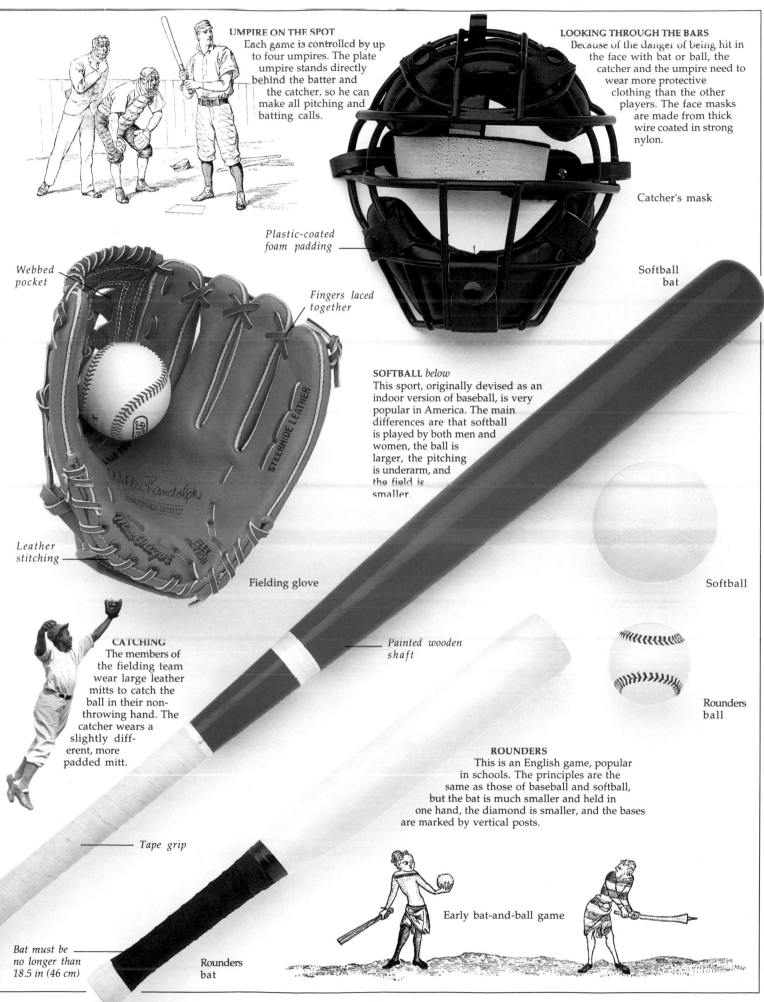

UMPIRE ON THE SPOT
Each game is controlled by up
to four umpires. The plate
umpire stands directly
behind the batter and
the catcher, so he can
make all pitching and
batting calls.

LOOKING THROUGH THE BARS
Because of the danger of being hit in
the face with bat or ball, the
catcher and the umpire need to
wear more protective
clothing than the other
players. The face masks
are made from thick
wire coated in strong
nylon.

Catcher's mask

*Plastic-coated
foam padding*

Softball
bat

*Webbed
pocket*

*Fingers laced
together*

SOFTBALL *below*
This sport, originally devised as an
indoor version of baseball, is very
popular in America. The main
differences are that softball
is played by both men and
women, the ball is
larger, the pitching
is underarm, and
the field is
smaller.

*Leather
stitching*

Fielding glove

Softball

*Painted wooden
shaft*

CATCHING
The members of
the fielding team
wear large leather
mitts to catch the
ball in their non-
throwing hand. The
catcher wears a
slightly diff-
erent, more
padded mitt.

Rounders
ball

ROUNDERS
This is an English game, popular
in schools. The principles are the
same as those of baseball and softball,
but the bat is much smaller and held in
one hand, the diamond is smaller, and the bases
are marked by vertical posts.

Tape grip

*Bat must be
no longer than
18.5 in (46 cm)*

Rounders
bat

Early bat-and-ball game

Cricket

CRICKET IS SIMILAR to baseball (p. 22), in the way teams take turns to bat and field. The two sports differ in that there are two cricket batsmen on the field at any one time and they must defend the "wicket" with their bat and score by running between the two wickets at opposite ends of the narrow "pitch". In addition, four runs are automatically scored if the ball is hit over the boundary of the field, and six if it crosses the boundary without touching the ground. Bat-and-ball games like cricket were probably played in England as long ago as the 13th century.

A gentleman cricketer

Wicketkeeper — *Wicket*

Batsman

THE FIELD
The cricket "pitch" is a narrow strip of short grass in the center of the field, 66 ft (20 m) long, with a wicket at each end. "Overs" (sequences of six balls) are bowled (pitched) from alternate ends.

Bowling "crease" (pitcher's boundary line)

Bowler

Umpire

Replica of an 18th-century bat

Screw-in spikes

SHOES
Many cricketers prefer to wear high-sided shoes with screw-in metal spikes. By tradition, most cricket clothing and footwear is white or off-white.

Wicketkeeper's gloves

Pimpled rubber

AN EARLY GAME
Cricket in the 18th century was played with five players on each team. There was only one wicket, and this had two stumps rather than three.

BOWLING
Cricketers bowl over-arm, and the ball bounces once before reaching the batsman. Slow bowlers spin the ball with their fingers so that it turns toward or away from the batsman, and faster bowlers bounce the ball off its raised seam to get a similar effect.

THE BALL
The cricket ball is made in a similar way to a baseball (p. 23) but is covered with red leather and has a straight-stitched seam.

Bails

Stumps

THE WICKETKEEPER
The wicketkeeper plays a similar role to the catcher in baseball (p. 21). Like the catcher, he wears leg guards because he is so close to the batsman. His well-padded gloves have pimpled-rubber palms to help grip the ball.

THE FIRST BATS
The word "cricket" may come from *cric*, the Old English term for a shepherd's crook, which the early cricket bats resembled. 18th-century bats were long and heavy with a curved blade. The modern style of straight bat was not used until the introduction of overarm bowling.

WICKETS
Modern wickets are made from ash, and are 28 in (71 cm) high. The wicket consists of three upright stumps and two bails which rest on the top. The batsmen is "bowled out" if the bowler (pitcher) knocks off one or both of the bails.

BATTING GLOVES
These protect the fingers from injury but allow enough freedom of movement to grip and wield the bat.

The weather vane depicting Old Father Time is a famous Lord's landmark

HAT TRICK *right*
Bowlers were once given hats if they "struck out" 3 batsmen in a row, hence the term "hat trick", used today if an ice hockey player scores 3 points in a game.

Modern cricket helmet

Protective plastic ear pieces

THE HOME OF CRICKET
Lord's cricket ground, known as the "home of cricket," was founded by Thomas Lord in 1787, and is the headquarters of the Marylebone Cricket Club (M.C.C.), which drew up the rules of the game. International matches are often played at Lord's; these last for five days and are known as "test" matches. The bat shown here has been signed by players taking part in a test match at Lord's.

COLORED CLOTHES
In floodlit cricket matches, each team wears a different-colored uniform. A white ball is used as it can be seen more easily.

Fastening straps

METAL BAT
An aluminum bat was used by a few players during the 1970s, but the fashion did not last long, as aluminum bats proved no substitute for the traditional wooden variety.

Metal bats were hollow inside

A MODERN BAT
Today's cricket bats are made from willow and have a cane handle, usually covered by a rubber grip. The average bat weighs about 2lb 5oz (1050 g) and is roughly half the weight of the old bat shown opposite.

LEG PADS *right*
These protect the shins of the batsman and wicketkeeper. The pads reach to the thigh, but still allow the batsman to run between the wickets. Batsmen can be "out" if they use their legs to keep the ball from hitting the wicket.

Ankle padding

How cricket bats are made

The introduction of fast overarm bowling in the early 19th century meant that batsmen needed lighter bats that could be swung more easily. The modern type of bat dates from that time, and despite various improvements in design, the style of the bat has changed little since then. The bat blade, which absorbs the impact of the ball, is made from willow, and the springy cane-and-rubber handle protects the hands from the shock of striking the ball.

THE TREE
Of the 36 varieties of English willow, only *Salix coerulea* and *S. virida* are suitable to be made into top-quality cricket bats. These are lightweight woods with a very straight grain.

USING THE WOOD
Each section of trunk is used to make between six and eight bats, depending on its size and quality.

W.G. GRACE
Probably the most famous of all batsmen is Doctor William Gilbert ("W.G.") Grace, who dominated the sport throughout the second half of the 19th century. During his career, he scored over 54,000 runs.

Rubber   *Cane*

Twine wrapped around handle

THE HANDLE
The handle is made from pieces of *Sarawak* cane formed into blocks with strips of rubber and bonded together tightly with strong glue.

1 SPLITTING THE TRUNK
Each 28 in (71 cm) length of willow trunk is cut into segments or "clefts"; then the bark is removed. The young outer "sapwood" is best for making bats; it is a lighter color than the inner "heartwood."

Sapwood

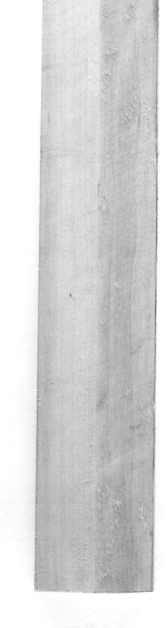

2 THE SEASONING PROCESS
The clefts are sawed into "blades," stacked, and left to dry for 2-4 weeks. Then they are put into a kiln to dry for a further 4-6 weeks.

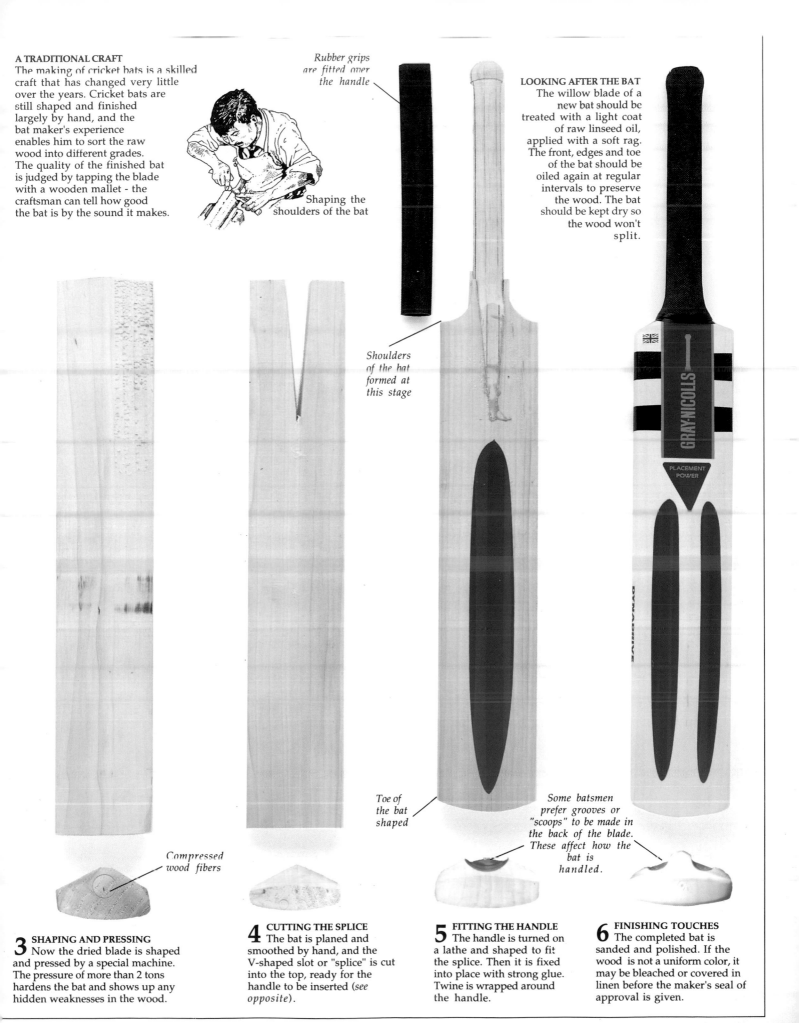

A TRADITIONAL CRAFT

The making of cricket bats is a skilled craft that has changed very little over the years. Cricket bats are still shaped and finished largely by hand, and the bat maker's experience enables him to sort the raw wood into different grades. The quality of the finished bat is judged by tapping the blade with a wooden mallet - the craftsman can tell how good the bat is by the sound it makes.

Rubber grips are fitted over the handle

Shaping the shoulders of the bat

LOOKING AFTER THE BAT

The willow blade of a new bat should be treated with a light coat of raw linseed oil, applied with a soft rag. The front, edges and toe of the bat should be oiled again at regular intervals to preserve the wood. The bat should be kept dry so the wood won't split.

Shoulders of the bat formed at this stage

Toe of the bat shaped

Some batsmen prefer grooves or "scoops" to be made in the back of the blade. These affect how the bat is handled.

GRAY-NICOLLS
PLACEMENT POWER
DYNADRIVE

Compressed wood fibers

3 SHAPING AND PRESSING Now the dried blade is shaped and pressed by a special machine. The pressure of more than 2 tons hardens the bat and shows up any hidden weaknesses in the wood.

4 CUTTING THE SPLICE The bat is planed and smoothed by hand, and the V-shaped slot or "splice" is cut into the top, ready for the handle to be inserted (*see opposite*).

5 FITTING THE HANDLE The handle is turned on a lathe and shaped to fit the splice. Then it is fixed into place with strong glue. Twine is wrapped around the handle.

6 FINISHING TOUCHES The completed bat is sanded and polished. If the wood is not a uniform color, it may be bleached or covered in linen before the maker's seal of approval is given.

Tennis

TENNIS IS PLAYED by two or four people on a court divided by a low net. Each player has a racket, and points are scored by hitting a ball over the net in such a way that it bounces inside the court and cannot be returned. "Real," or Royal, tennis originated in France during the Middle Ages and was very popular among the European noblemen of the 16th century, but it was not until the 19th century that "lawn tennis" was first played. The sport quickly became very popular with both men and women. Today tennis is played on clay, cement, wood, and plastic courts, as well as on grass.

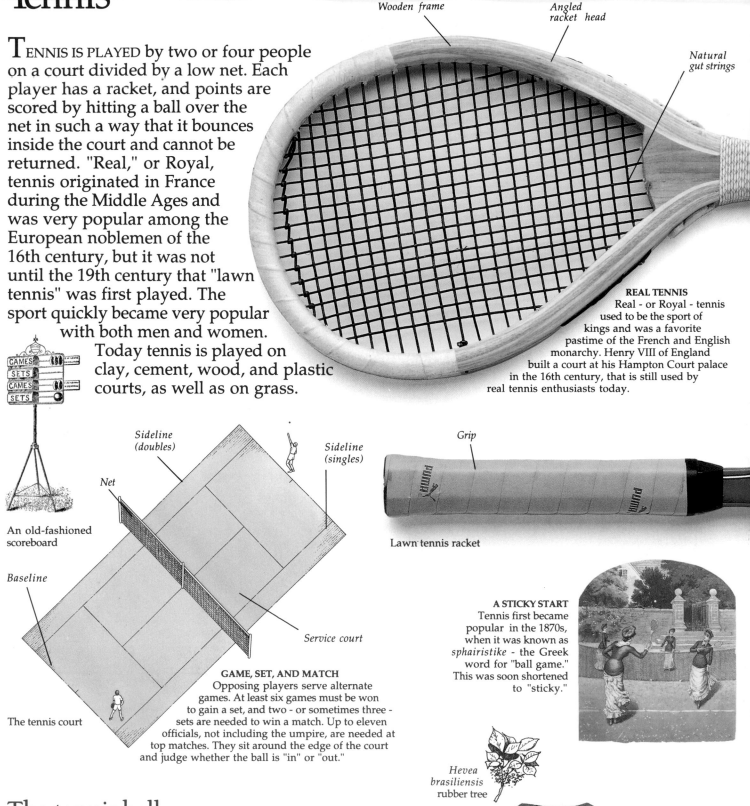

Wooden frame

Angled racket head

Natural gut strings

REAL TENNIS
Real - or Royal - tennis used to be the sport of kings and was a favorite pastime of the French and English monarchy. Henry VIII of England built a court at his Hampton Court palace in the 16th century, that is still used by real tennis enthusiasts today.

An old-fashioned scoreboard

Sideline (doubles)

Net

Sideline (singles)

Baseline

Service court

The tennis court

Grip

Lawn tennis racket

GAME, SET, AND MATCH
Opposing players serve alternate games. At least six games must be won to gain a set, and two - or sometimes three - sets are needed to win a match. Up to eleven officials, not including the umpire, are needed at top matches. They sit around the edge of the court and judge whether the ball is "in" or "out."

A STICKY START
Tennis first became popular in the 1870s, when it was known as *sphairistike* - the Greek word for "ball game." This was soon shortened to "sticky."

Hevea brasiliensis rubber tree

The tennis ball

The progression from real tennis, played on indoor courts, to lawn tennis, played in the gardens of "polite society," was not as obvious as it may seem. Indeed, before it was possible at all, somebody had to invent a ball that would bounce on grass!

REAL FAILURES
The traditional real tennis balls were made from sheepskin and filled with sawdust, sand, or wool. They did not bounce on grass.

RAW RUBBER
Latex (rubber) comes from the stems of certain trees. It was not until the 19th century that rubber-tree seeds were brought to Europe and grown commercially.

CLOISTER COURT
Real tennis courts have gallery "roofs" jutting out around three of the four sides, and points are won according to how the ball is hit into and through the galleries. The strange design of the court is like the monastery cloisters where the game was first played.

IN THE CHAIR
The tennis umpire sits in a high chair next to the net so he has the best possible view of the match. He announces the score after each point has been played.

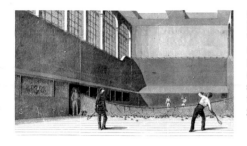

Real tennis racket

WIMBLEDON
The oldest and most important tennis championships are held at the All England Tennis and Croquet Club, Wimbledon, London. The first championships were held in 1877.

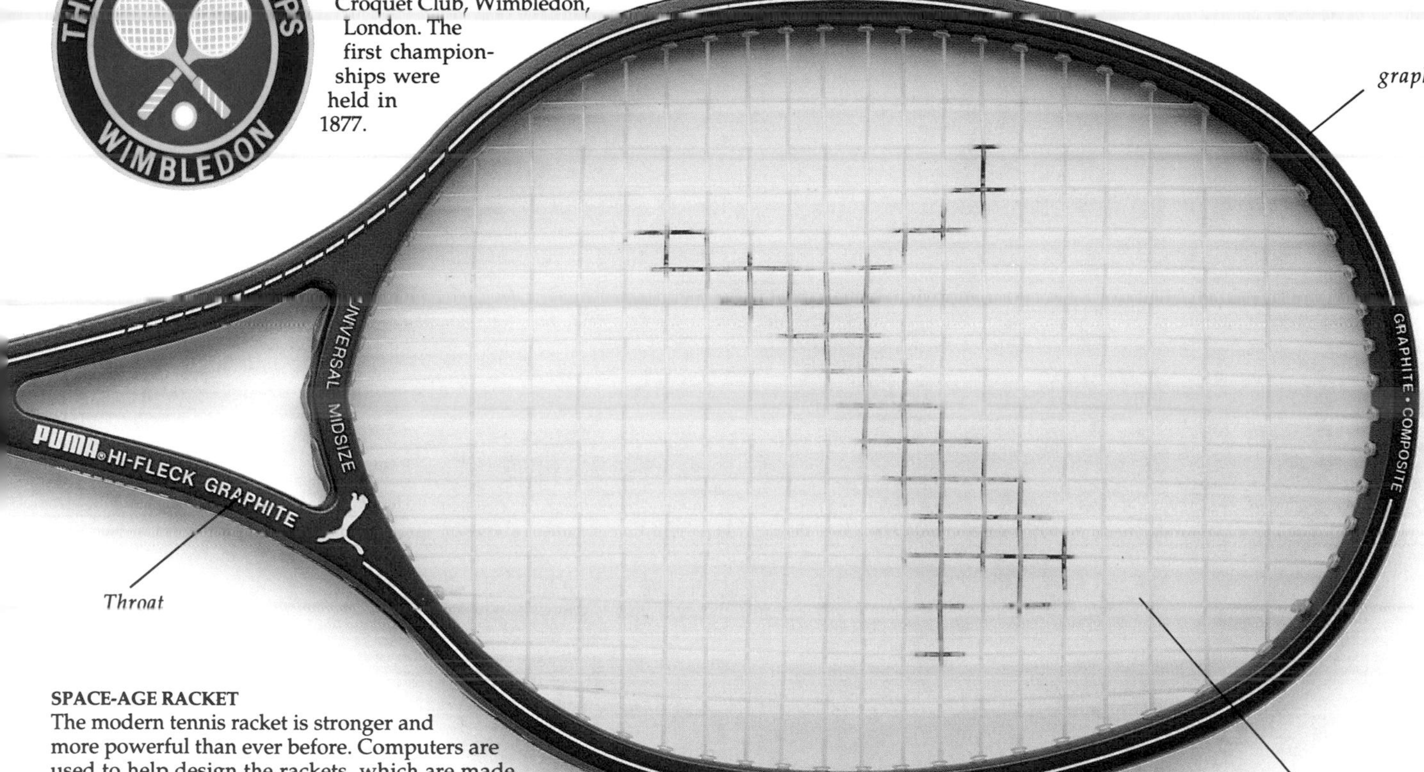

Molded graphite frame

PUMA® HI-FLECK GRAPHITE

UNIVERSAL MIDSIZE

GRAPHITE · COMPOSITE

Throat

SPACE-AGE RACKET
The modern tennis racket is stronger and more powerful than ever before. Computers are used to help design the rackets, which are made from materials developed for the aerospace industry.

Synthetic strings

Head

HOW THE BALL IS MADE
The rubber is "vulcanized" (treated with sulfur at high temperatures) to make it stronger and more elastic. The hollow ball is formed from two halves bonded together.

THE COVERING
The plain rubber ball was rather slippery in wet conditions, so a flannel covering was invented. Modern balls are covered with a mixture of wool and man-made fibers.

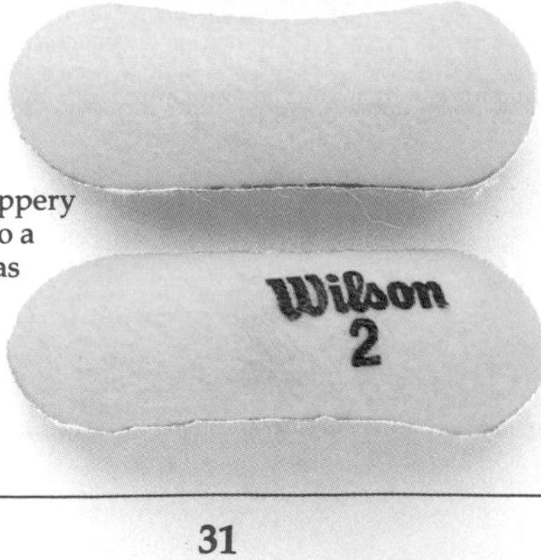

Wilson 2

BALL CHANGES
The pressure inside the ball changes in different conditions and during play, so the balls used in major matches are kept refrigerated at 68°F (20°C), and replaced after every few games.

Wilson 2

Tennis rackets

The sport we know today as tennis can be traced back to the French game of *Jeu de Paume*, in which two players hit a ball to each other with the palm of their hand. Soon, pieces of wood and webbed gloves started to be used instead, and by the start of the 15th century, strung "rackets" had been invented. Today's rackets are the result of trial and error over the years; until very recently, there were no rules governing the design and proportions of the racket, and many different styles and materials have been used during the past 100 years. Different kinds of stringing have also been tried - even wire "strings" were used at one stage.

International Tennis Federation rules now state that the overall dimensions of any racket must not exceed 32 in (81.28 cm) in length and 12.5 in (31.75 cm) in width, and that there must only be one set of strings on each racket.

Woman player of 1890

Aluminum frame

Piano-wire strings

Solid ash frame

1900s *below*
By the early years of the 20th century, the familiar symmetrical (even) shape of the racket had been introduced. A popular feature of the period was the "fishtail" handle - considered to be the height of fashion. Grooves were often cut into the handle to improve the grip.

FIRST METAL RACKET *right*
During the 1920s, experimental rackets with aluminum frames were made. The fact that they were strung with piano wire did nothing for their appeal, as it meant that the wool-covered tennis balls quickly wore out.

1920s *above*
Leather grips were introduced around this time to make the racket much easier to hold. Most racket frames were still being made from a solid piece of ash, but the shafts were becoming narrower and the edges more rounded to reduce wind resistance.

Leather grip

Symmetrical head

Fishtail handle

Grooved grip

1880s *below*
The first lawn-tennis rackets were similar to those used in real tennis, with uneven pear-shaped heads. They weighed much the same as modern rackets but the natural gut was much coarser and strung more loosely than today.

Plain wooden handle

Uneven head

1930s *below*
The "Hazell's Streamline" racket has an unusual handle, designed to reduce wind resistance, and a laminated (layered) head. Using thin layers of different woods, rather than a solid piece, means the racket is lighter, stronger, and cheaper to make.

Laminated frame

Reinforced shoulders

Streamlined handle to reduce wind resistance

Forehand ground stroke

Backhand volley

Serve

USING THE RACKET
To achieve the maximum control over each stroke, the racket must travel exactly along the direction and height the player wishes the ball to go, but the racket is used in a different way for each type of shot. Ground strokes involve swinging the racket, whereas the volley needs a punching technique; the serving action is one of "throwing" the racket at the ball, and the lob is a scooping stroke.

Forehand lob

Double stringing

1950s *above*
This classic wooden racket was the most popular design for two decades. The frame has multiple laminations of ash and other woods that are used for decoration and to make the racket stronger. The "shoulders" are reinforced for added strength.

Narrow aluminum frame

Molded graphite frame

1970s *above*
This decade saw the appearance of improved metal rackets. These could be made with a narrower frame than wooden rackets of the same strength, which meant they could travel faster through the air. Some rackets were double-strung to give extra spin to the ball (double stringing has since been banned).

1980s *above*
Nowadays, top-class players don't use wooden rackets and very few use metal ones. Instead, racket frames are molded from a combination of materials such as carbon graphite, fiberglass, boron, and ceramic.

33

Table tennis and badminton

T ABLE TENNIS AND BADMINTON are indoor sports in many ways similar to tennis. Badminton is played with a feather "shuttlecock" on a court with a high net, and table tennis is played with a light-weight ball on a rectangular table with a low net. Both sports date from the 1870s. The first "table tennis" match was between two British university students, using cigar boxes as bats and a champagne cork as a ball!

PING-PONG SET
The sport was also known as "Ping-Pong" because of the sound the ball made when it was hit with the paddle. It was a popular social activity around the turn of the century, when boxed Ping-Pong sets were sold in stores.

Paddle faces were made of parchment

Paddles had long wooden handles

PRICE FOURPENCE.
HOW TO PLAY
PING-PONG.
WITH DIAGRAMS
AND LAWS.

Early net with brass posts

HOW PADDLES ARE MADE *below*
The blade of the paddle is made of plain wood, but this must be covered with pimpled rubber. The pimples may face inward or outward depending on the desired effect on the ball, but must be evenly spaced on the rubber.

Plywood blade of even thickness

THE GRIP
Some players prefer to hold the paddle as if it were a pen.

White celluloid ball

Outward-facing pimples

Inward-facing pimples

Cellular rubber

Rubber must be one color only.

MODERN PADDLE
The sport became much more interesting in the 1920s, when the paddle was given a studded rubber face that enabled a player to put spin on the ball.

1901 MATCH *left*
Plain wooden paddles made for long, boring rallies, and the popularity of table tennis declined until rubber-faced paddles were introduced.

Badminton

Question: Which international sport is named after somebody's house? Answer: Badminton, called after the ancestral home of the Duke of Beaufort in Gloucestershire, England. The sport is thought to have been adapted from a children's game as an after-dinner entertainment for the duke's guests.

Rigid wooden frame

1880s racket

Service court

Short service line

THE COURT
This is similar to a tennis court but with a higher net. Points are won when the shuttle-cock touches the ground inside the court.

Long service line (doubles)

Long service line (singles)

Flexible frame bends along whole length of racket to give extra power to shots

1980s racket

EARLY AND MODERN RACKETS
The early wooden racket is similar to a tennis racket of the same period but is much lighter and more delicate. Modern rackets are made from new materials that are light, flexible, and strong. The shape of the racket head has changed completely.

SERVING
The shuttlecock is dropped, and then hit from below the waistline. The head of the racket must be below the server's hand when the shuttle is hit.

Plastic shuttlecock

SHUTTLECOCKS
The shuttlecock, in various forms, has been a popular toy around the world for many years. Those used in badminton are usually made with 14-16 goose feathers; plastic shuttles are used too.

Goose feathers

Ball-bearing weight

Feather shuttlecock

Cork base

RETURNING SERVE
The racket is held high to hit the shuttle as early as possible.

BATTLEDORE AND SHUTTLECOCK
The original parlor game, as played in the 18th century, was noncompetitive and consisted simply of hitting the shuttlecock back and forth with the "battledore" (or bat).

Squash and racketball

Squash, or "squash rackets," is one of several sports played on a court with four walls; others include rackets, fives, paddleball, racketball, and court handball. One player hits the ball against the front wall, and the other tries to return it before it has bounced more than once on the floor. The old game of rackets was first played in the 18th century in Fleet Prison, London; the inmates took to hitting a ball against the prison walls as a way of passing the time. A hundred years later, rackets players at Harrow School, England, invented squash as a practice game, its name coming from the soft or "squashy" ball that was used. Like the other racket sports, squash and racketball can be played by two (singles) or four players (doubles). In America, squash is played on a narrower court and with a much harder (almost solid) ball.

Protective strip prevents damage to the racket head

Each racket has about 27 ft (8.2 m) of string

| Yellow dot (very slow) | White dot (slow) | Red dot (fast) | Blue dot (very fast) |

COLOR-CODED BALLS
Temperature and other weather conditions affect the performance of the hollow rubber ball. Squash balls are made in four varieties - ranging from very slow for hot conditions to very fast for cold conditions. The different kinds of ball are coded with colored dots. Most top players use the very slow ball, which has a less pronounced bounce.

Squash racket

THE RACKET
Squash rackets have a smaller, rounder head than those used for badminton or tennis. Like other rackets, most modern squash rackets are now made from materials such as carbon graphite and fiberglass. Some rackets have a frame with a hollow core that reduces racket vibration when the ball is hit.

Synthetic strings

STRINGS
For all racket sports, the choice of strings is very important, as the string is the only part of the racket that actually touches the ball. Nowadays synthetic strings are popular with many players; each string may have up to 48 individual plastic strands, or "filaments," and many are coated with silicone and nylon to protect them from dirt and moisture. Natural gut strings are still widely used too - these are more "elastic" than synthetic strings, so they are strung less tightly on the racket.

Natural gut strings

SPECTATOR SPORT
The development of glass and plexiglass walls meant that an audience could watch a match from all sides of the court. This made squash much more popular as a spectator sport.

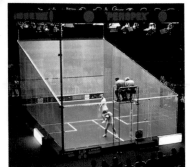

Squash court with plexiglass walls

EYE PROTECTORS
Some players wear special shatterproof goggles to protect their eyes in case they are struck by the fast-moving ball.

Racketball

This very modern relative of squash was first played in the United States during the early 1950s. It evolved from court handball and, more directly, from paddleball - in which players used wooden bats, or paddles, rather than strung rackets. As with squash and badminton, points can only be won when a player is serving. When the server loses a rally, his opponent earns the right to serve. The winner is the first player to score 21 points.

Racketball racket

THE BALL
The hollow rubber ball is larger than a squash ball. When dropped from a height of 100 in (2.5 m), it must bounce 68-72 in (1.7-1.8m) in a temperature of 76°F (24.5°C).

Racketball glove

THE RACKET
The racket has a slightly larger head than a squash racket, but the handle is much shorter. Some players use a wrist thong attached to the end of the handle.

FAST AND FURIOUS
Squash and racketball are two of the fastest and most energetic of all sports. Good players must be very fit and agile. Players must be ready to play within 10 seconds of the end of the previous rally, and are penalized if they try to delay the game longer in order to regain their strength.

Wrist thong

LEATHER GLOVE
Players may wear a glove on their racket hand to get a better grip on the handle. The sheepskin used for this glove has been treated to make it "tacky."

Squash/racketball shoe

JAI ALAI
This sport, which comes from northern Spain, is played on a long, narrow court by players holding curved baskets, or *cestas*, made from woven reed and attached to a leather glove.

Basque jai alai player

INSIDE A SHOE
Modern sports shoes of all kinds are designed to be strong, light, and comfortable. Shoes worn by racket-sports players have to be well padded to avoid jarring the heels and ankles, and ventilated to allow the feet to "breathe."

Padded foam tongue for comfort

Reinforced heel gives support

Rubber soles provide sure grip

Thick sole absorbs shock

Athletics

THE VARIOUS SPORTS that make up athletics are divided into two main groups: track events (running and walking) and field events (jumping and throwing). These are among the earliest and most basic forms of testing speed, strength, agility, and stamina, and can be traced back directly to the ancient Greek games, some 4,000 years ago. Most athletes only do one or two events, but a few choose to compete in a range of track and field events, the *heptathlon* for women (seven events held over two days) and the *decathlon* for men (ten events over two days).

Hollow relay batons

TEAM EVENT
The relay is the only athletics event in which teams compete directly against each other. A baton is passed between four team members, who each run either 100 m or 400 m.

Starting pistol

Blanks

FROM START TO FINISH
Races are started by firing a starting pistol. In top-class meetings, this triggers a highly accurate electronic timing device; ordinary stopwatches are used in lower levels of competition. The athlete is judged to have finished the race when his torso (not his arms, legs, head, or neck) crosses the line.

Track events

Races of up to one lap in length are run in eight lanes. Because the distance around the outside of the track is greater than the inside, the athletes start in a staggered line so that each one runs an equal distance.

1,500 m start

5,000 m start

200 m start

Staggered starts

Lanes

100 m start

400 m start

Finishing line (all races)

Stopwatch

Olympic torch-bearer

THE OLYMPIC GAMES
The Olympics are held every four years, and include athletics and a great variety of different sports. The Olympic symbol of five interlocking circles represents the five participating continents of the world.

The Olympic symbol

ON THE BLOCKS *left*
Sprinters use starting blocks that are fixed to the track. They provide a firm base for the foot to push against at the start of the race. Blocks can be connected to a device that detects any false starts - when an athlete's foot leaves the blocks before the gun goes off.

CROSS-COUNTRY RUNNING
As well as track events, there are long-distance races run on roads and across country. Such courses may include obstacles like fences, ditches, and streams.

38

ROAD RUNNING SHOES
Road runners' feet undergo an enormous amount of stress during each race, so their shoes must give support and be very comfortable.

Screw-in spikes

Air-cushioned sole

QUICK MARCH
Walkers differ from runners in that they must have at least a part of one foot in contact with the ground at all times. Walking races are usually over longer distances than running races.

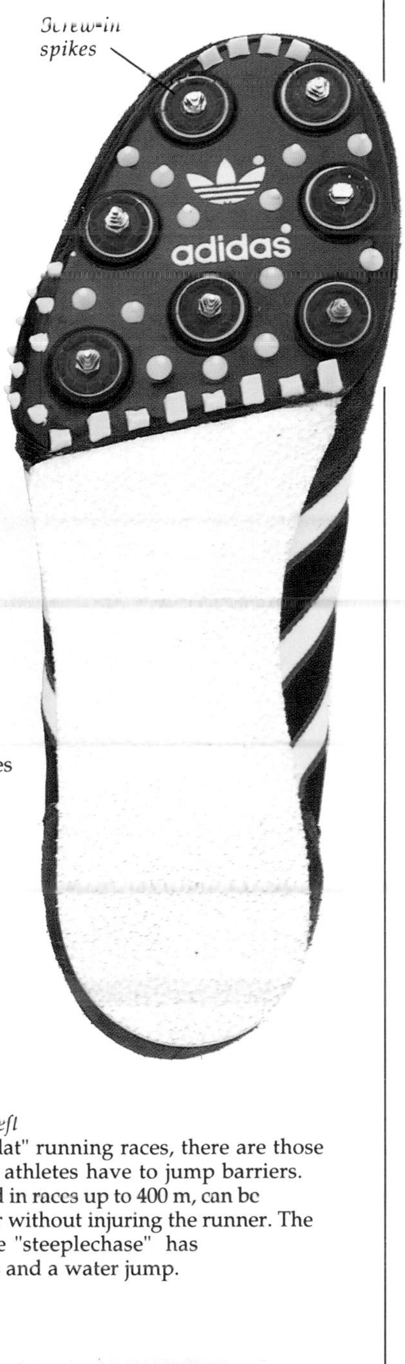

Track shoes

TRACK SHOES *above*
Athletes who race on the track use tight-fitting, lightweight shoes with spiked soles. The spikes provide the best grip on the track and allow sprinters to reach speeds of up to 25 mph (40 kmh).

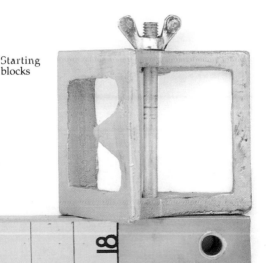

Starting blocks

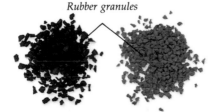

HURDLING *left*
As well as "flat" running races, there are those in which the athletes have to jump barriers. Hurdles, used in races up to 400 m, can be knocked over without injuring the runner. The long distance "steeplechase" has solid barriers and a water jump.

Rubber granules

TYPES OF TRACK
Older tracks are made from grass or cinders; modern tracks are made from synthetic rubber and polyurethane materials and are used for training and racing in all weathers.

Cross-section of synthetic track

The springy texture of a synthetic track means that athletes can run faster than on other surfaces

Shot is made from iron or other hard metal. Those for indoor use are rubber filled with lead pellets

Men's shot
16 lb (7.26 kg)

PUTTING THE SHOT
The shot is a heavy, cannonball-like ball. It is held in one hand against the side of the chin and propelled by pushing (or "putting") it away from the body - actually throwing it is against the rules. As in all throwing events, different weights are used for men and women and for different age groups.

Women's shot
4 kg (8lb 13oz)

THE HAMMER
The hammer weighs the same as the men's shot, but the addition of the wire and the different throwing technique mean that it can be thrown four times as far. Because the hammer has been known to land on the track, the event is now usually held at a different time from the other events. Women do not compete in the hammer event.

Hammer-throwing technique

Measuring tape

THROWING THE HAMMER
The thrower swings the hammer around his head several times and then rotates his whole body before releasing the handle.

Hammer

THE JAVELIN
Javelin-throwing contests are among the oldest of all sports. The throwing action is similar to that used by spear-carrying huntsmen. The javelin can be thrown farther than the shot, hammer, or discus. The men's javelin weighs 800 g (28.22 oz) and the women's javelin 600 g (24.74 oz).

Aluminum shaft

Javelin

Spear-throwing huntsman

THE HIGH JUMP
Most high-jumpers use a technique called the "Fosbury flop," in which they jump the bar "backward." This style of jumping is named after the American athlete Dick Fosbury, who invented it.

BEST FOOT FORWARD
Throwers and jumpers usually wear different shoes than runners do, often with heel spikes. High jumpers sometimes wear one spiked shoe and one training shoe.

Cord grip

Heel spikes

High-jump shoes

Field events

The field events take place in the area enclosed by the track, although the runways for the long jump, triple jump, and pole vault are sometimes situated outside the track. The hammer and discus are thrown from inside a wire safety cage to protect spectators from wayward throws.

MEASURE OF SUCCESS
Throws and jumps are measured from that part of the mark which is nearest to where the jump or throw was made.

Point of javelin must land first for throw to count

Shot circle

Javelin runway

Triple-jump runway

Hammer/discus cage

Hammer wire

High-jump "fan" (runway)

Long-jump runway

Pole-vault runway

THE POLE VAULT *below*
Improvements in equipment have helped athletes to vault higher and higher over the past hundred years. The vaulters of a century ago used poles made of hickory or ash, with a steel spike on the end, and had only a sandpit to land in. Today's fiberglass poles are stronger and more flexible than wooden poles, and modern vaulters have deep, padded mats to land on.

THE DECATHLON
The decathlon is a combination of four track events, three throwing, and three jumping events. On the first day, the competitors take part in the 100 m, the long jump, the shot, the high jump, and the 400 m. The second day begins with the 110 m hurdles, followed by the discus, pole vault, javelin, and 1,500 m.

THE DISCUS
Discus throwing was one of the original Olympic contests. The discus is made of wood or plastic with a rounded metal rim. Modern discuses weigh 2 kg (4.5 lb) for men and 1 kg (2.25 lb) for women.

Wire twisted through loop in handle

Hammer handle

1.5 K

Criterion

Discus

Ancient Greek discus thrower

THE LONG JUMP AND TRIPLE JUMP
Long- and triple-jumpers run up to a take-off board and jump into a pit filled with sand. The triple jump used to be called the hop, step, and jump. Women do not compete in this event.

Triple-jump technique

Hop

Step

Jump

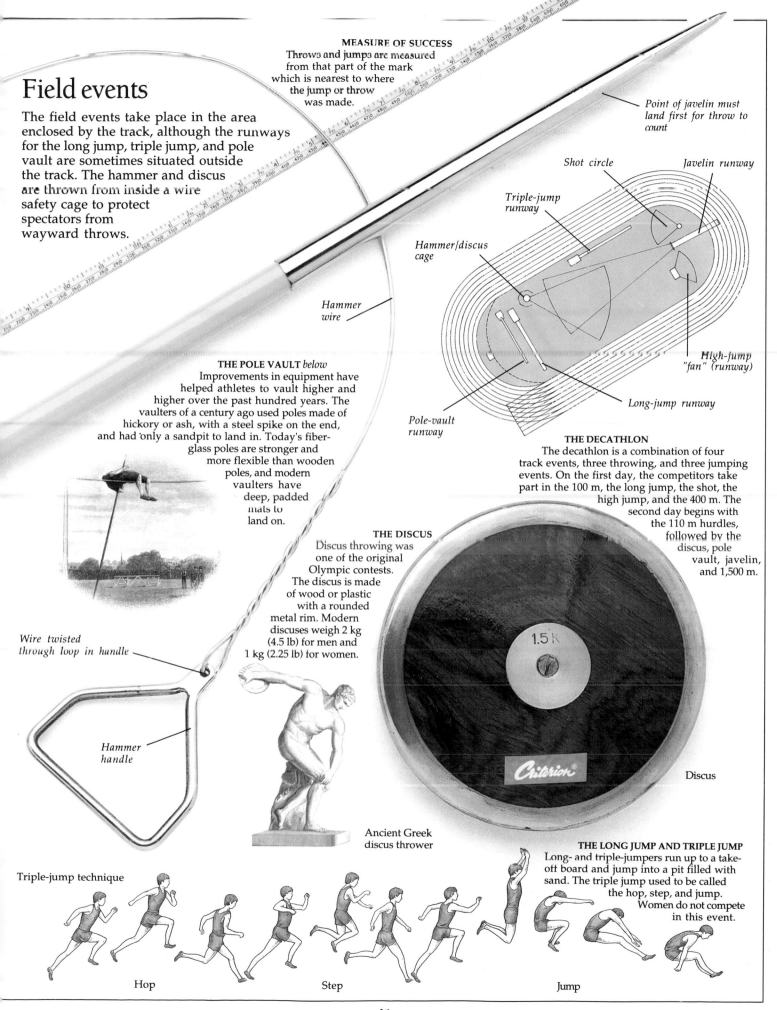

Gymnastics

GYMNASTICS IS A MIXTURE of different events, testing strength, agility, coordination, and balance. Gymnasts use standard apparatus (equipment) on which they perform a series of exercises that are marked by judges. Men compete in six events: the rings, pommel horse, parallel bars, high bar, vault, and floor exercises. Women also compete in the vault and floor exercises, as well as on the beam and uneven parallel bars. Many modern gymnasiums have other kinds of equipment that people can use to keep fit.

RIBBON RHYTHM
The floor exercises are performed on a marked-out area 40 ft (12 m) square. Gymnasts must make use of this whole area but are not allowed to step outside it. The exercises consist of tumbling, jumping, and balancing movements; women's floor exercises may be accompanied by music. A recent variation on the sport is "rhythmic" gymnastics, in which female gymnasts perform floor exercises with ribbons, balls, hoops, ropes, and Indian clubs.

HANGING AROUND
The rings are suspended 8ft 2in (2.5 m) from the ground. All the movements must be performed without making the rings swing back and forth on their frame.

Wooden rings are 7 in (18 cm) in diameter

PARALLEL BARS *below*
Movements performed on the parallel bars have names such as "peach basket" and "elephant lift." The record number of parallel bar "dips" (push-ups) is over 700 in a 30-minute period.

WALKING THE PLANK
Gymnasts do somersaults, cartwheels, and turns on the beam, which is 16.5 ft (5 m) long and 4 ft (120 cm) off the ground. Performing on the beam is a real balancing act, as it is only 4 in (10 cm) wide.

HIGH BAR
Exercises on the high bar must consist of nonstop swinging movements, with backward and forward swings and changes of grip. As with other events, the high bar is judged according to how difficult the exercises are and how well they are performed.

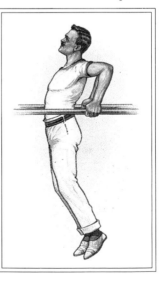

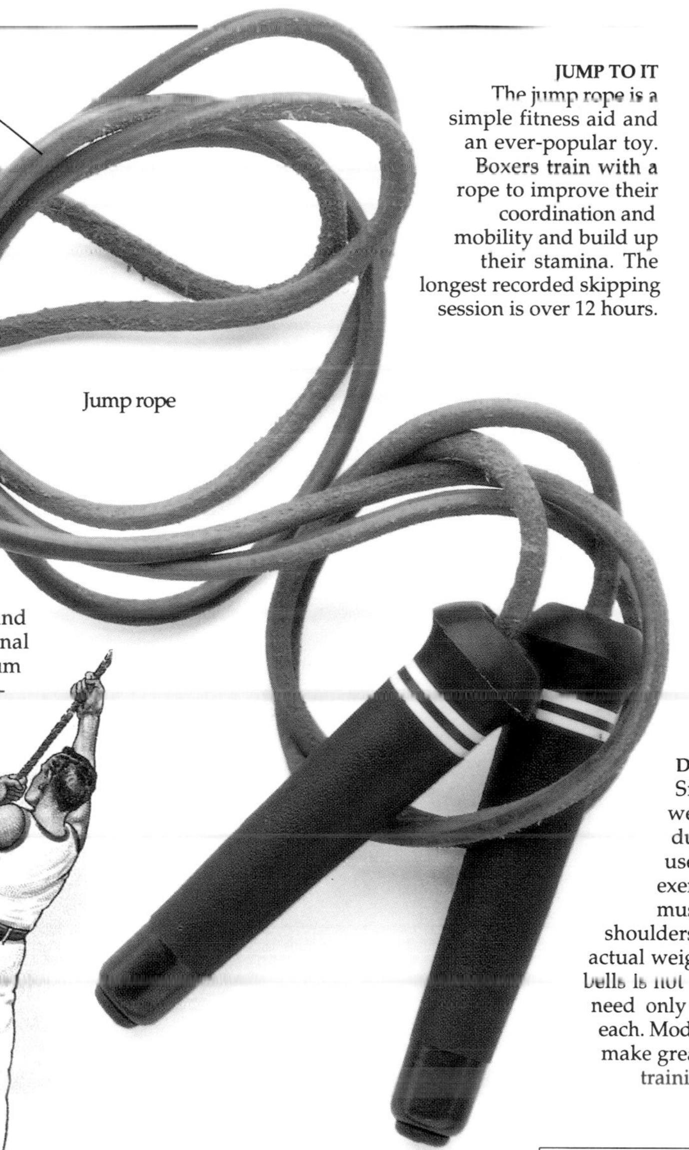

Leather "rope"

Jump rope

JUMP TO IT
The jump rope is a simple fitness aid and an ever-popular toy. Boxers train with a rope to improve their coordination and mobility and build up their stamina. The longest recorded skipping session is over 12 hours.

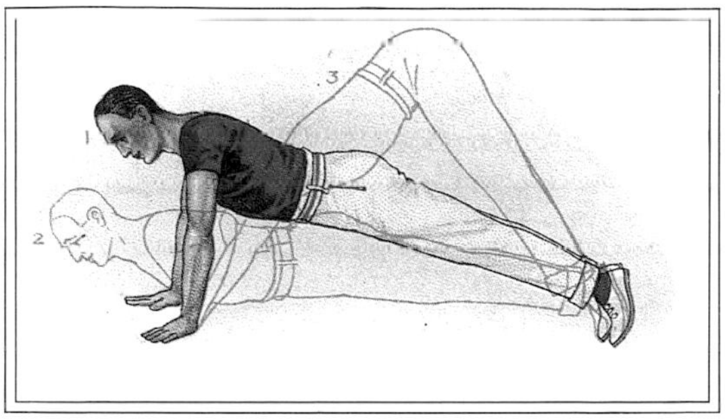

ROPE CLIMBING
Climbing frames and ropes are traditional pieces of gymnasium equipment. Climbing strengthens the arm muscles and promotes agility and coordination.

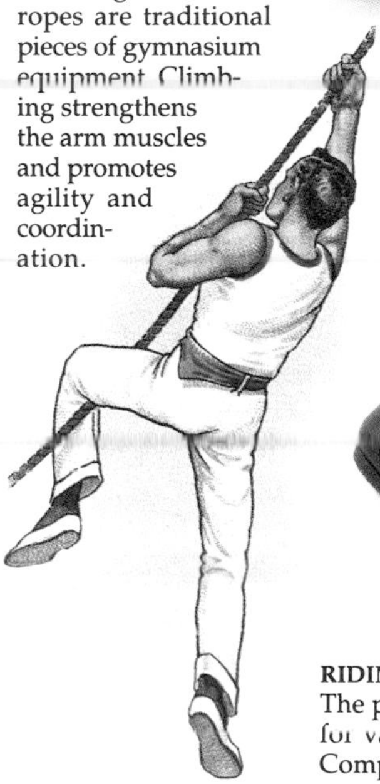

RECORD PUSH-UPS
Push-ups (or "press-ups") are a very basic exercise to build up stamina and strength in the muscles of the arms and chest. The greatest non-stop push-up sequence is over 32,000, and over 3,000 have been done using one arm only.

Vinyl dumbbell

DUMBBELLS *right*
Small, hand-held weights are called dumbbells and are used in a variety of exercises to build up muscles in the arms, shoulders, and chest. The actual weight of the dumbbells is not important - they need only weigh 2 lb (1 kg) each. Modern gymnasiums make great use of weight-training as a means of exercise.

RIDING A HORSE *below*
The pommel horse is similar to the one used for vaulting but has two handles attached. Competitors perform a series of swinging movements, using all parts of the horse and keeping their feet and legs away from it.

NOUANSPORT

Dumbbell exercise to strengthen shoulders

BENDY BARS *below*
This "power twister" is one of the many simple fitness devices designed to exercise muscles in all parts of the body.

How the power twister is used

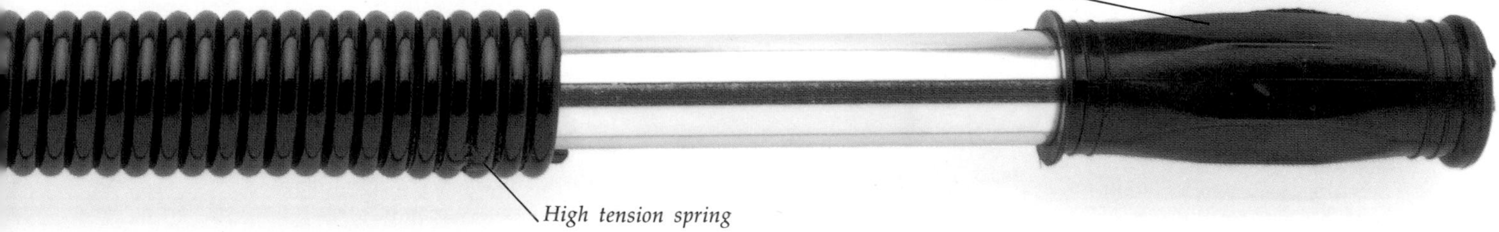

Handles

High tension spring

Weightlifting

THE LIFTING OF WEIGHTS is one of the oldest and most simple forms of testing strength. Modern weightlifters compete against each other according to their body weight, as heavier men can usually lift the larger weights. In recent years, a great many people have discovered how training with weights helps build up the strength and stamina needed in other sports. Others use weights to develop muscles "for their own sake" and compete in special bodybuilding contests.

DISK WEIGHTS *below*
These cast-iron disks range from 0.25 kg (0.5 lb) up to 25 kg (56 lb), so that any weight can be added to the bar by a combination of disks. The greatest weight ever raised by a human is 6,270 lb (2,844 kg), equal to the combined weight of three dozen fully grown men.

1.25 kg
(2.75 lb)

2.5 kg
(5.5 lb)

CIRCUS STRONGMAN *left*
The modern form of weightlifting, using a bar and weighted disks, only dates from the end of the last century. Before then, strongmen performed great lifting feats as part of circus and fairground shows.

Weight-training gloves

BACK SUPPORT *above*
Lifters use wide belts to protect their backs from injury.

MUSCLE POWER
Male and female bodybuilders train with weights in order to make their muscles as big as possible. Then they oil their bodies to make the muscles stand out even more, and parade in front of judges in special bodybuilding contests.

Female bodybuilder

Metal ridge to keep weights from sliding inward

Hand grips

Rough-textured metal where bar is gripped by lifter

LOADING THE BAR
The disk weights are attached to a bar that is 7ft 4in (220 cm) long and weighs 20 kg (44 lb). The weight of the bar forms part of the total weight lifted. The largest weights are always on the inside and the smallest on the outside. This is so gradual increases in the weight can be made quickly after each successful lift.

"Clean"...

CLEAN AND JERK
One of the standard weightlifting techniques is the two-part "clean and jerk," where the bar is first lifted onto the chest and then, when the lifter has steadied himself, pushed up over the head in a separate action. The lifter must "lock" his elbows and knees to complete the lift.

...and "jerk"

5 kg
(11 lb)

7.5 kg
(16.5 lb)

10 kg
(22 lb)

COLLARS
There are various types of collar that are used to hold the weights securely on the bar.

Spring collar

Quick-release collar

Screw-on collar

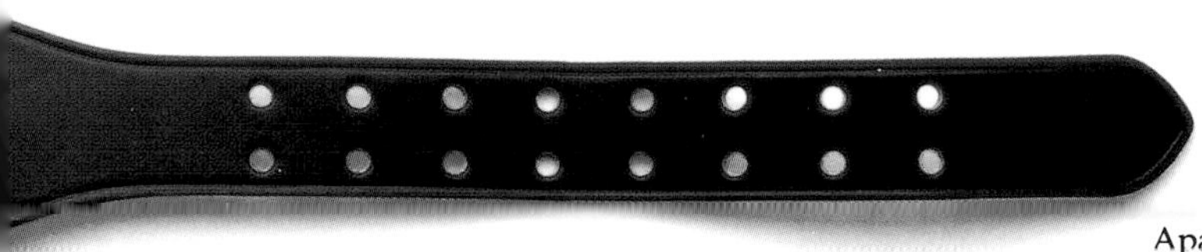

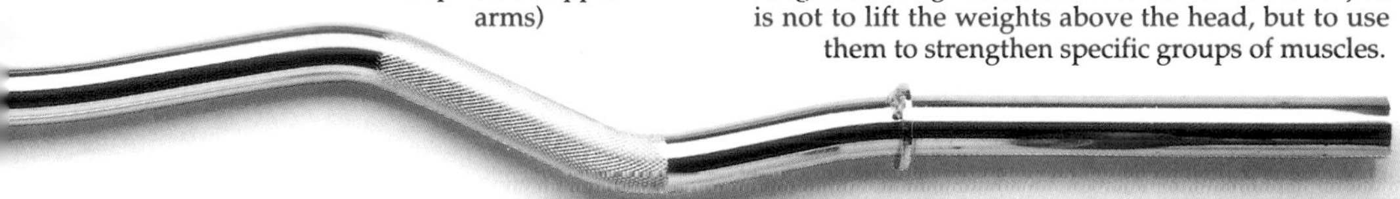

Bar for exercising biceps (front upper arms)

Bar for exercising triceps (rear upper arms)

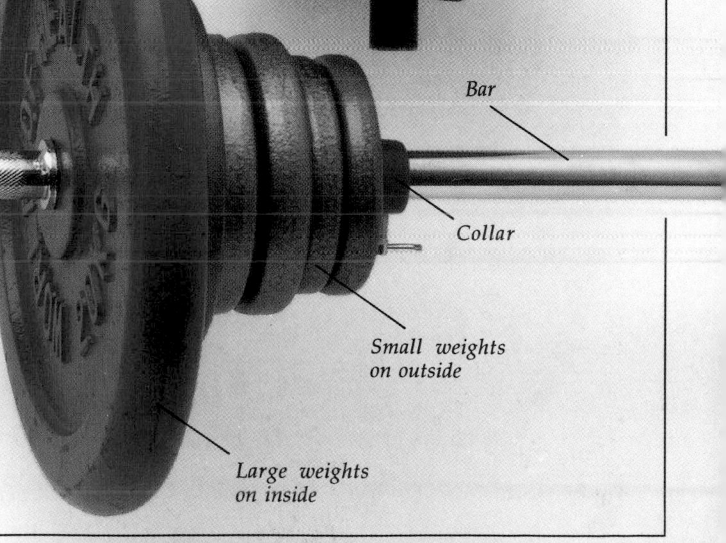

PLASTIC WEIGHTS *right*
Rubber- or plastic-covered weights are normally used in top-class competitions. These are usually color-coded according to weight. The 50 kg (110 lb) weights, which are green, are only used if there is no other way of loading all the weight onto the bar.

These plastic-covered dumbbell weights are filled with sand

TYPES OF BARS *below*
Apart from the standard straight bar, different-shaped bars are used for various weight-training exercises. In these cases, the object is not to lift the weights above the head, but to use them to strengthen specific groups of muscles.

Bar

Collar

Small weights on outside

Large weights on inside

SNATCH *right*
The other type of lift is called the "snatch," in which the bar is hoisted above the head in one movement. It is much harder to lift heavy weights in this way. Contests are decided by adding up the weights lifted in the snatch and the clean and jerk.

POWERLIFTING
Powerlifters can lift much heavier weights than other weightlifters as they do not have to raise the bar above their heads.

45

Boxing

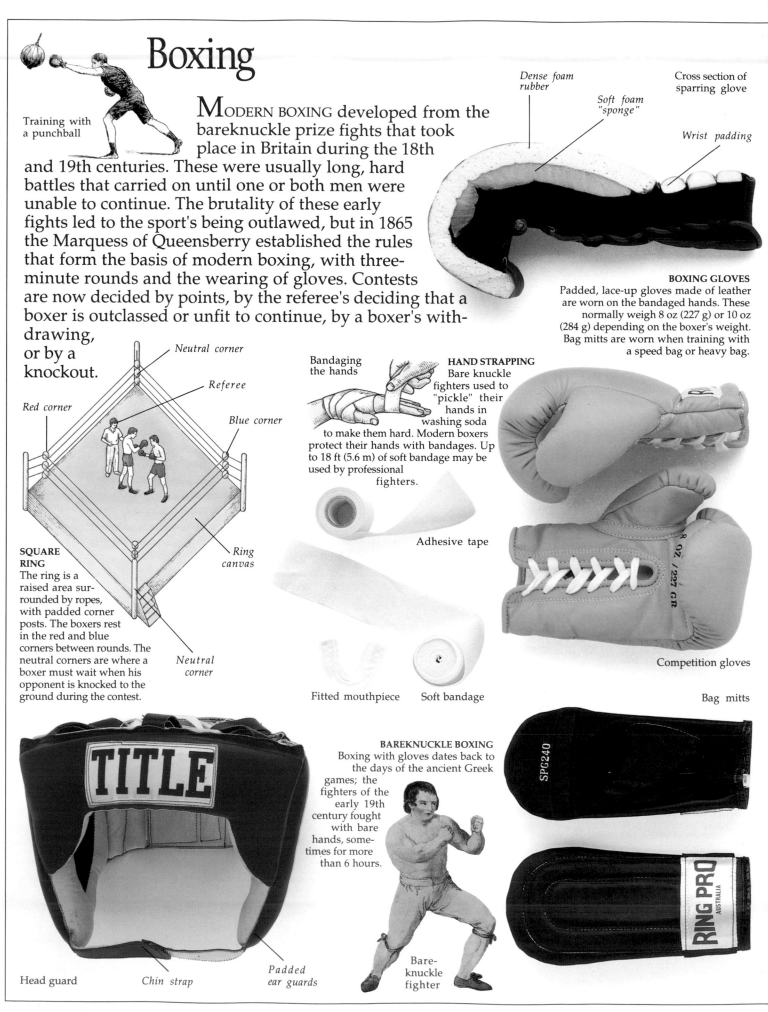

Training with a punchball

MODERN BOXING developed from the bareknuckle prize fights that took place in Britain during the 18th and 19th centuries. These were usually long, hard battles that carried on until one or both men were unable to continue. The brutality of these early fights led to the sport's being outlawed, but in 1865 the Marquess of Queensberry established the rules that form the basis of modern boxing, with three-minute rounds and the wearing of gloves. Contests are now decided by points, by the referee's deciding that a boxer is outclassed or unfit to continue, by a boxer's withdrawing, or by a knockout.

Dense foam rubber

Soft foam "sponge"

Cross section of sparring glove

Wrist padding

BOXING GLOVES
Padded, lace-up gloves made of leather are worn on the bandaged hands. These normally weigh 8 oz (227 g) or 10 oz (284 g) depending on the boxer's weight. Bag mitts are worn when training with a speed bag or heavy bag.

Neutral corner

Referee

Red corner

Blue corner

Ring canvas

SQUARE RING
The ring is a raised area surrounded by ropes, with padded corner posts. The boxers rest in the red and blue corners between rounds. The neutral corners are where a boxer must wait when his opponent is knocked to the ground during the contest.

Neutral corner

Bandaging the hands

HAND STRAPPING
Bare knuckle fighters used to "pickle" their hands in washing soda to make them hard. Modern boxers protect their hands with bandages. Up to 18 ft (5.6 m) of soft bandage may be used by professional fighters.

Adhesive tape

Fitted mouthpiece

Soft bandage

Competition gloves

Bag mitts

TITLE

Head guard

Chin strap

Padded ear guards

BAREKNUCKLE BOXING
Boxing with gloves dates back to the days of the ancient Greek games; the fighters of the early 19th century fought with bare hands, sometimes for more than 6 hours.

Bareknuckle fighter

SPG240

RING PRO
AUSTRALIA

Elasticized belt

AMATEUR OR PROFESSIONAL? *above*
Amateur fights are fought over three rounds of three minutes each, compared to up to 15 rounds for professional championship bouts. Amateurs always wear singlets and the protective headguard that professionals use only when sparring (practicing). Every boxer wears a mouthpiece, molded to the shape of his mouth, to protect his teeth. A lace-up protector is worn under the trunks to guard against any stray punches.

Boxing club emblem embroidered on trunks

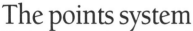

BOXING TRUNKS
Boxers wear loose fitting trunks. Those used for professional fights are traditionally made from satin and often have the name of the fighter or his initials embroidered on them. The "belt" is the line between the top of the boxer's hips and his navel, and this must be shown by a clear contrast in color. Deliberately hitting "below the belt" is against the rules.

Boxer's initials

The points system

The judges award points to each boxer at the end of every round. The maximum number of points per round (20) is given to the boxer who has been most skillful in landing his punches during that round; after an equal round, both boxers might get 20 points. To score points, a punch must be made with the knuckle part of the glove on the front or sides of the opponent's head or upper body. At the end of the last round, the man with the highest total of points is declared the winner.

Direct left-hand blow to the body

FANCY FOOTWORK
The ability to move quickly and smoothly around the ring is an important aspect of boxing. Fighters practice their "dancing" with a jump rope as part of their training. The tall boxing shoes are light-weight and have a thin sole with no heel.

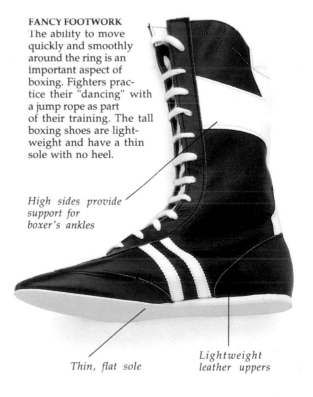

High sides provide support for boxer's ankles

Thin, flat sole

Lightweight leather uppers

Ducking to avoid left-hand punch and countering with right-hand blow to jaw

Ducking to the right avoids left-hand blow to the head

47

Martial arts

MARTIAL ARTS are those skills that are used in battle and therefore include fencing, shooting and archery, as well as the sports described here. However, the term is usually used to describe the various combat sports that come from the Far East, of which judo and karate are the most widely practiced. *Judo* means "the soft way" and involves throwing and holding movements. *Karate*, on the other hand, means "empty hand" and is a mixture of punching and kicking techniques. The martial arts were first practiced by the ancient Japanese samurai warriors, who were armed with bows and swords. The unarmed combat techniques, from which modern judo and karate evolved, enabled the warriors to continue fighting if they were suddenly disarmed by their opponent.

Film fighter Bruce Lee helped make the martial arts popular in the 1970s

KUNG FU WEAPONS
As well as the various forms of unarmed combat, martial artists learn to master weapons such as the *nunchaku*, two wooden handles joined by a metal chain. This weapon developed from a tool used in the Chinese rice fields. Nunchakus with safe rubber handles are used in sporting competitions

Nunchaku

KENDO *below*
The traditional Japanese art of *kendo* is a form of fencing with wooden swords. The competitors, or *kendoka*, wear traditional padded clothing. Each bout lasts for just 3-5 minutes.

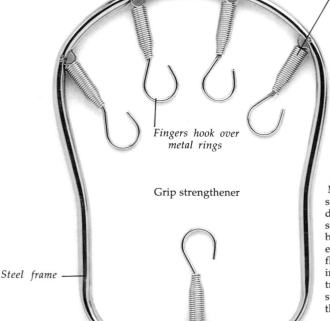

Leather hilt

Shinai

Round "tsuba," or shield, is made of leather

SUMO WRESTLING
The origins of Japanese *sumo* wrestling, in which contestants try to push each other out of the ring, date back to the 1st century B.C. The wrestlers put on weight by eating a high-protein stew - the heaviest wrestler on record was 496 lb (225 kg). Ritual is an important part of the sport.

Strong metal springs

Fingers hook over metal rings

Grip strengthener

GRIPPING STUFF
Martial arts fighters are supremely fit. Various devices, such as this grip strengthener, are used to build up strength and endurance. Agility and flexibility are also important - fighters train with special leg-stretchers that help them kick higher.

Steel frame

KENDO EQUIPMENT
The *kendoka* wear protective masks, gloves, breastplates, and aprons. The kendo sword is called a *shinai* and is made from four strips of bamboo lashed together with string and leather. It must be less than 47 in (118 cm) long.

Leather tip

Bamboo strips

SELF-DEFENSE
Judo, karate, and the other martial arts are practical forms of self-defense, as well as competitive sports.

Red belt
9th-11th *dan*

Judo
Judo students are trained to make use of an opponent's strength to overcome him, while saving their own energy. Sporting bouts are strictly controlled, and the object is to display superior technique rather than to injure the opponent. Different levels of points are awarded according to the standard of throwing and holding movements.

Black belt
1st-5th *dan*

Brown belt
1st *kyu*

"Semicontact" gloves

KARATE GLOVES
The many different forms of karate have different rules about the amount of physical contact allowed and the protective clothing worn by the contestants. Various gloves are sometimes used in practice and in competitions.

SMASHING TECHNIQUE
The special physical and mental training of karate fighters enables them to break slabs of concrete and blocks of wood with their hands, feet, or head.

Blue belt
2nd *kyu*

Green belt
3rd *kyu*

Karate
Karate contests usually last two minutes and are controlled by a referee and four judges. Actual physical contact is not required to score points - as with judo, it is superior technique that counts.

Orange belt
4th *kyu*

Foot protectors

FOOT PROTECTORS
These padded shoes slip over the bare feet of the fighter to protect them when he kicks at an opponent.

JUDO BELTS *right*
Fighters are awarded colored belts to show the grade they have reached. The highest level reached by most people is the black belt, but there are three levels above this - red-and-white striped, red, and white belts.

Yellow belt
5th *kyu*

Fencing

FENCING IS A COMBAT SPORT using swords and takes place on a narrow *piste* (strip) 14 m (46 ft) long. The winner is the fencer who scores the greater number of "hits" on his opponent. The three types of modern sword - the *foil*, *épée*, and *saber* - are descendants of the *rapier*, which was a popular court weapon in the 16th century. The rapier and dagger replaced the heavier sword and "buckler" (shield) that had been carried before. Fencing swords do not have cutting blades, and the tip is formed into a blunt button to prevent injuries.

16th-century duelist

METAL JACKET
In some contests electronic equipment is used to show when a hit has been scored. Fencers have to wear special jackets covering the target area; these are made from woven metal threads that conduct the electricity, so the scoreboard lights up when they are touched by the tip of the sword.

MESH MASK
The traditional mask protects the face and head, and a padded bib protects the throat. The fine mesh is made from stainless steel or molded plastic. It allows the fencer to see out but prevents any accidental injuries to the eyes.

CLOTHING
The fencer's clothes must allow him freedom of movement and give maximum protection. They must be white and made from stong material, and there must be no fastenings in which a sword may become caught.

GAUNTLET
A long white glove, or gauntlet, is worn only on the sword hand. It is slightly padded and extends halfway up the fencer's forearm.

Guard

Insert brass screw

Steel foil pommel

Leather pad

"Tang"

Blade

Alternative "pistol-grip" handle

THE BLADE
The blade is square in cross section and has a groove running along its whole length. In electric-sword contests, the wire runs down this groove and is taped into place.

THE SWORD
Swords are subject to strict rules governing their design and safety. The total length of any type of sword must not be more than 44 in (110 cm) - 42 in (105 cm) for the saber.

Gripping the handle

THE SABER
The saber may have a straight or curved blade; any curve must be continuous and less than 1.5 in (4 cm). The sword must weigh less than 1 lb (500 g) and the guard must measure no more than 6 in x 5.5 in (15 cm x 14 cm). Unlike the other swords, the edges of the saber - as well as its tip - can be used to register hits.

The target area in saber competitions is the trunk and arms

THE FOIL
This light sword was developed specially for fencing practice in the 18th century. It weighs the same as the saber, but its guard must have a diameter of no more than 4.5 in (12 cm). In electric foil contests, a hit registers only when pressure on the point is at least 1 lb (500 g).

The target area for foil is the trunk, not including the arms

THE EPEE
This is the traditional dueling sword, heavier than the foil and saber, with a maximum weight of 1.5 lb (750 g) and a guard no larger than 5.5 in (13.5 cm) in diameter. A pressure of 1.5 lb (750 g) is needed to score a hit in electric épée bouts. Foils and épées usually have a strap, called a martingale, attaching the sword to the fencer's hand.

The target area for épée is the whole of the opponent's body

DUELISTS
The sport of fencing developed directly from the use of the sword in warfare and dueling. Gentlemen used to fight duels regularly as a way of settling "matters of honor," but these resulted in so many deaths that they were banned in many countries. Duelists often carried a sword in one hand and a dagger in the other.

SWORD HILTS
The hilt (handle) of the modern sporting saber most closely resembles those of dueling swords, which were designed to protect the sword hand.

Modern saber hilt

16th-century rapier hilt

CAVALRY CHARGE
The saber used in modern fencing competition is a light version of the sword used by cavalry troops in the 18th and 19th centuries. The weapon was specially designed for use by troops on horseback and had a flat, curved blade.

Martingale

USING ELECTRICITY
Official foil and épée competitions now use an electric scoring system in which the sword tips are connected to lights by a long wire that passes underneath each fencer's jacket.

Counter of Quarte

Counter of Sixte

Counter of Septime

Counter of Seconde

FENCING TECHNIQUE
These circular movements - which are made by moving the fingers and wrist only - are used to deflect the opponent's blade. Many of the fencing terms date from the 16th or 17th century, when the light court sword was introduced in France.

Button

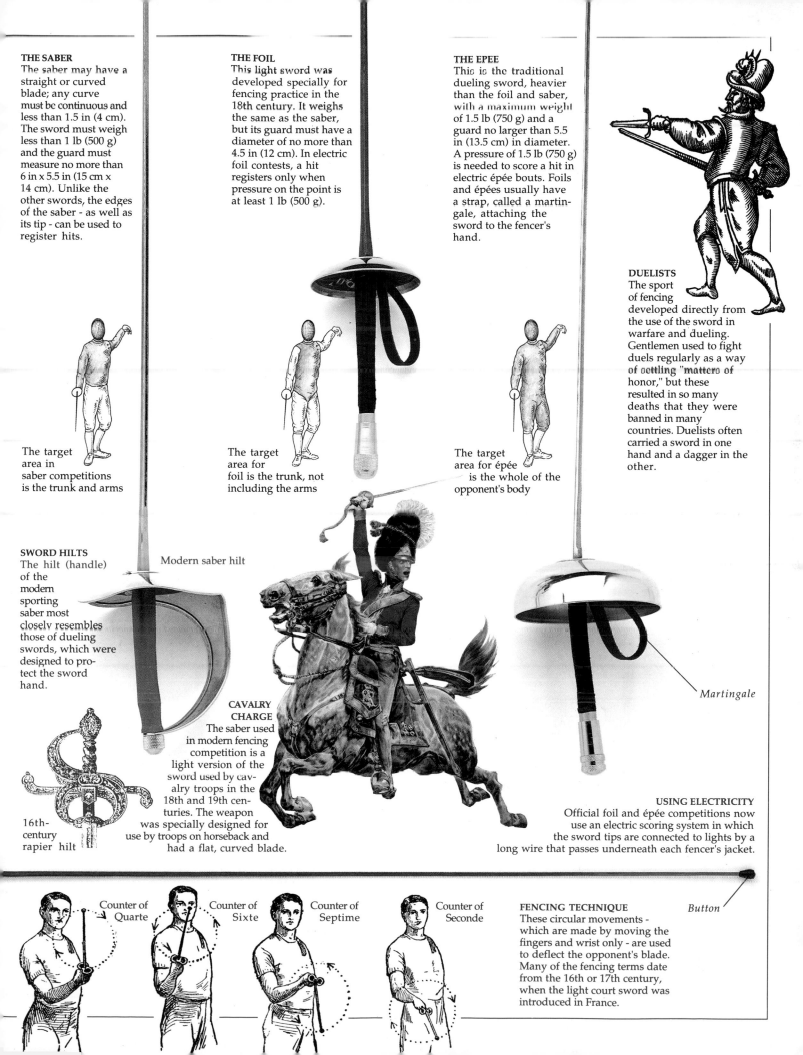

Archery

Cupid's arrows cause people to fall in love

VARIOUS FORMS of bow and arrow have been used to fight battles and as hunting tools for thousands of years. Modern sporting bows are designed and made according to the same principles, although the sights, stabilizers, and other attachments make them look very different. Competitors in target archery shoot a certain number of arrows at targets fixed at different distances - 30 m, 50 m, 70 m, and 90 m for men, and 30 m, 50 m, 60 m, and 70 m for women. The points scored are added up to give a total, and the archer with the highest total is the winner. Crossbows are sometimes used in separate competitions.

THE BAYEAUX TAPESTRY
Archers and slingers used to be less effective in battle than an army's main forces of cavalry and infantry (foot soldiers), until the introduction of the longbow in the Middle Ages.

PROTECTION
A "bracer" is worn on the arm that holds the bow, to protect it against the bowstring. A glove or finger tab is worn on the drawing hand.

Finger tab

Archer's glove

Bracer

The Dacron string is taken off the bow after each shooting session

Hardwood laminate (layered) limbs

"Riser"

THE MODERN BOW
Until recently, bows were always made from wood, the best being yew. Modern bows are usually made from laminates and other materials, such as fiberglass and carbon. These are much stronger and therefore more reliable.

Magnesium handle

STABILIZERS *below*
These are screwed into the "risers" to make the bow more stable while shooting so each shot is consistent.

"V-bar" stabilizers

VICTORIAN ARCHERS
The bows used by 19th-century British archers were usually made from two pieces of wood spliced (joined) together in the center. Those made from a single piece are called "self bows".

Sight ring attachment

BOWSIGHT *left*
A sight can be fixed to the side of the bow to help the archer concentrate his or her aim.

The "nock" rests on the string

There are three feather "fletches" on each arrow

HUNTING WEAPON *left*
Like many other weapons, the bow and arrow was first used to help man catch his food. In the case of the Indians, it was used to kill buffalo, which also provided hides to make clothing and shelter.

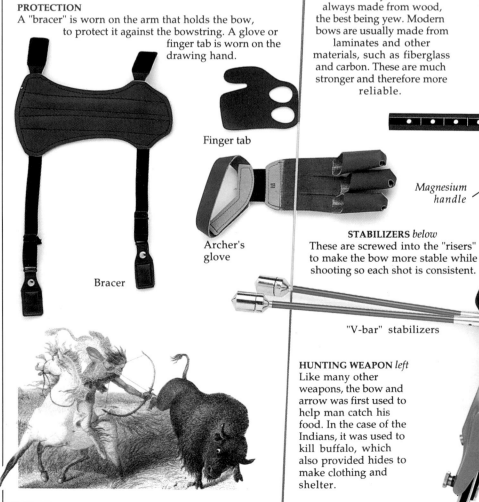

MINI ARROWS
Crossbows fire "bolts," which are much shorter than arrows but must be at least 12 in (30 cm) long.

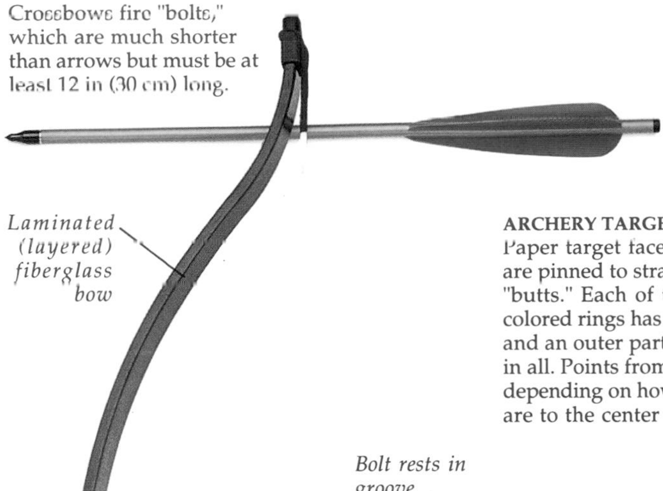

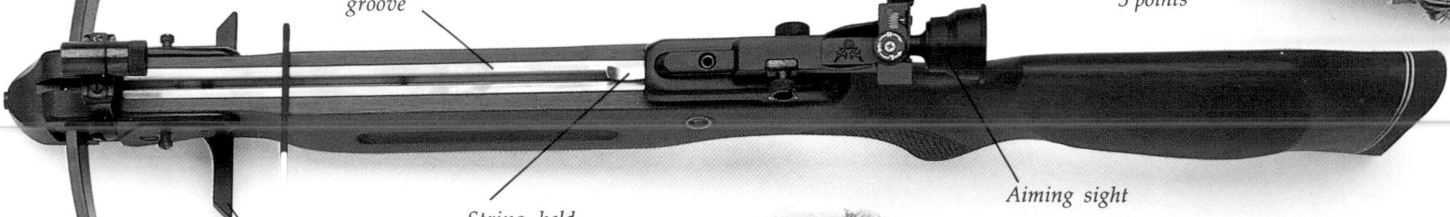

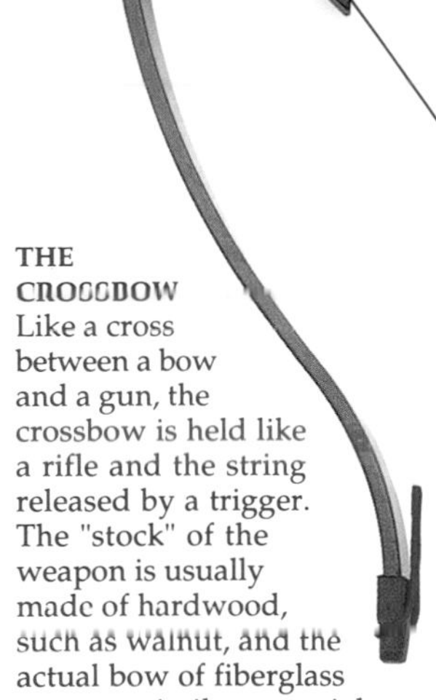

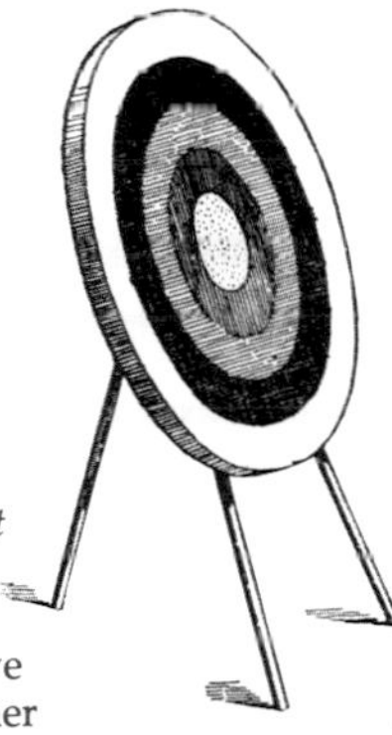

Laminated (layered) fiberglass bow

ARCHERY TARGET *right*
Paper target faces are pinned to straw "butts." Each of the five colored rings has an inner and an outer part, making ten areas in all. Points from 1 to 10 are scored depending on how close the arrows are to the center of the target - the bull's-eye.

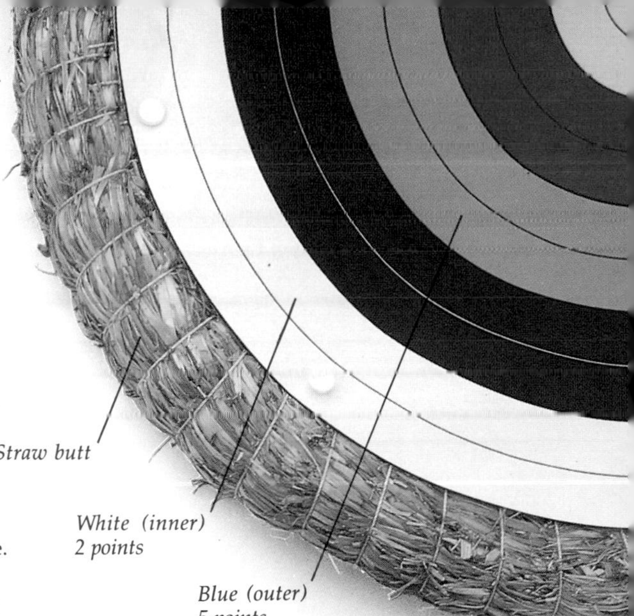

Straw butt

White (inner) 2 points

Blue (outer) 5 points

Bolt rests in groove

Aiming sight

String held back in firing position here

Stirrup held between feet when drawing bow

THE CROSSBOW
Like a cross between a bow and a gun, the crossbow is held like a rifle and the string released by a trigger. The "stock" of the weapon is usually made of hardwood, such as walnut, and the actual bow of fiberglass or some similar material.

WILLIAM TELL
The legendary Swiss hero William Tell was ordered to shoot an apple off his young son's head as a punishment. The legend usually says that he used a crossbow, but this picture shows him with a longbow.

Metal tip

THE PARTS OF AN ARROW *above*
The craft of making arrows is known as "fletching." Cedar and pine are the woods traditionally used to make the best arrows.

Wooden shaft

THE QUIVER *right*
This is the "holster" that holds the arrows. It is usually worn on a belt around the archer's waist. The arrows in this quiver have aluminum shafts and plastic fletches.

LONGSHOT *left*
Modern bows are very powerful. A "footbow," in which the arrow is drawn back with both hands, can shoot an arrow well over a mile. The record for a handbow is over 3,600 ft (1,100 m).

Aluminum long-rod stabilizer

Shooting

LIKE ARCHERY, the sport of shooting grew out of the use of weapons as hunting tools. Indeed, sporting shotguns are still used today for shooting small game (birds, rabbits, and so on), as well as the so-called clay pigeons. Rifles are used in target shooting and to hunt deer and other big game. Shooting competitions differ according to the type of firearm and ammunition used, the position of the marksman, and the form of the target.

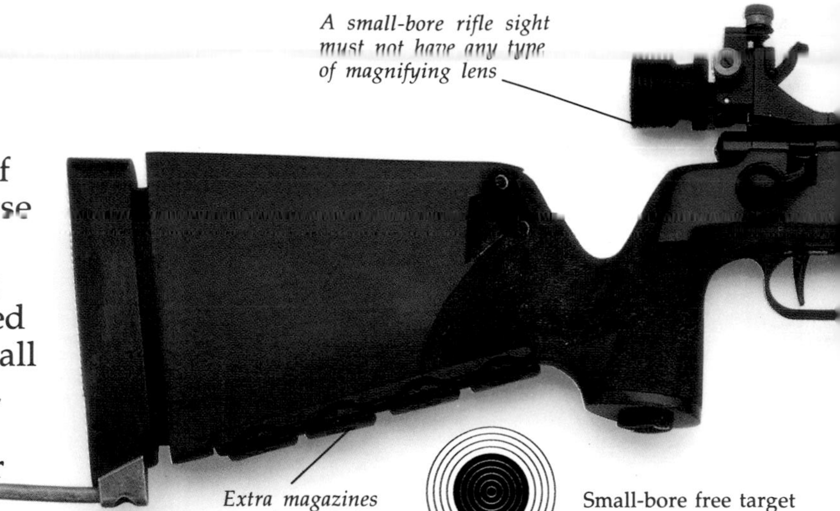

A Wild West trick shooter

A small-bore rifle sight must not have any type of magnifying lens

Extra magazines stored in rifle butt

Small-bore free target

Telescopic sight

BIG-BORE AMMUNITION *left*
These bullets, also used to hunt deer and other big game, are 0.3 in (7.62 mm) caliber. They can travel up to 2 miles (3.2 km) when fired.

RAPID-FIRE PISTOL SHOOTING *below*
There are various pistol-shooting competitions: the main one is the rapid-fire event over 25 m (83 ft). A row of five silhouette targets is turned to face the competitor for just 4, 6, or 8 seconds, during which he must fire one shot at each of them.

Target pistol

0.35 in (9 mm) ammunition

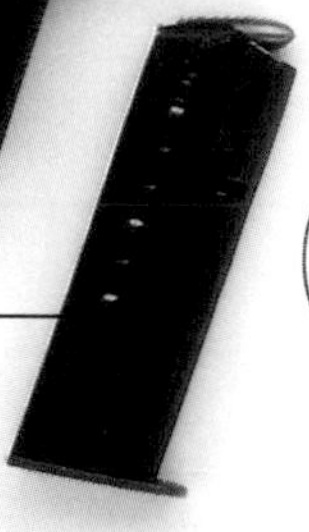

Standard 20-yard pistol target

HELPING HEARING
Competitors in all top shooting events wear head-phone-style ear protectors.

Magazine with ammunition

OVER-AND-UNDER GUN *above*
This gun is called a shotgun, because it fires a mass of tiny pellets, or "shot," instead of bullets. The shot is contained in a cardboard cartridge that is ejected from the barrel after firing. The twin barrels are placed one over the other.

Rapid-fire pistol

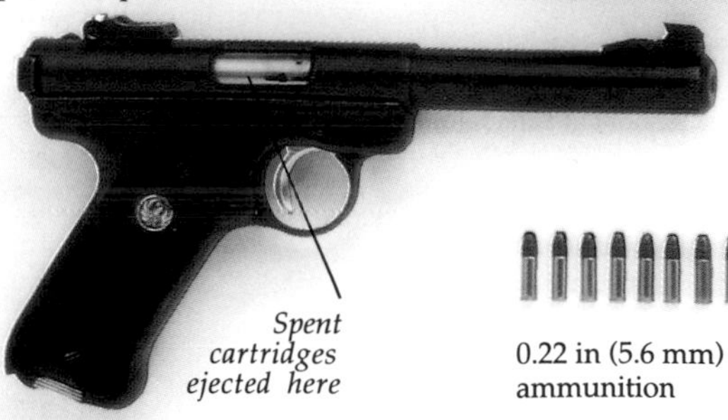

Spent cartridges ejected here

0.22 in (5.6 mm) ammunition

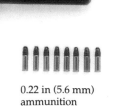

Rapid-fire target

SMALL-BORE FREE RIFLE *below*
This weapon is fired from a distance of 50 m (165 ft) at a round target 6.5 in (16.24 cm) across. The diameter, or "caliber," of the bullets used is 0.22 in (5.6 mm).

Barrel sight

Ammunition for small-bore free rifle

THE BIATHLON
This is a modern sport combining cross-country skiing and rifle shooting. Competitors ski a course of up to 20 km (12.5 miles) and stop for three or four sessions of shooting at targets from a range of 150 m (495 ft).

ANNIE GET YOUR GUN
The remarkable Annie Oakley was a famous trick shooter: as part of her act, she would shoot a cigarette from between the lips of her husband and split a playing card from a distance of 30 paces.

BIG - BORE RIFLE *above*
This hunting rifle is fired over a distance of 1,000 ft (305 m) at a target 39 in (1 m) across. The term "rifle" refers to the spiral groove inside the barrel of the guns that causes the bullets to spin through the air as they are fired.

Air-pistol pellets

Over-and-under barrels

AIR WEAPONS
Air pistols and rifles use compressed air or carbon dioxide to fire tiny pellets from a range of 10 m (33 ft) at targets just 1.8 in (4.6 cm) across. These pellets have to be loaded one at a time.

The wooden grip is specially shaped to fit the hand exactly

Cartridge

Pellets

"BB" 4.3 mm
(0.172 in)
shot

"No. 9" 2.0 mm
(0.08 in)
shot

TYPES OF SHOT
Different sizes of shot are used for different purposes. Large pellets travel farther and are used to shoot birds; smaller pellets scatter over a wide area more quickly and are used in clay-pigeon shooting.

CLAY PIGEONS
These small, saucer-shaped clay disks are launched two at a time from special traps on the ground, and their flight resembles that of game birds.

A traditional hunting scene *left*

SIDE-BY-SIDE GUN *above*
This traditional sporting gun is used to shoot small game birds. Its barrels are alongside each other rather than "over and under." Special "gun dogs" are trained to retrieve birds that have been shot by their masters.

Bowling sports

THERE ARE TWO main kinds of bowling sports: those in which the object is to knock down pins or skittles, and those in which the players try to get their bowls (balls) nearer to the target ball, or "jack," than their opponent. Modern tenpin bowling was "invented" when the game of skittles - which had nine pins arranged in a diamond formation - was banned in some states in the 1840s; the players merely added another pin and put them all in a triangle.

Crown-green bowls jack

Boule

BOULES *above*
The sport of boules, or pétanque, is played mainly by the French. The heavy metal spheres are rolled or thrown at a small wooden jack. The field usually has a sandy surface.

Boules technique

Bowls technique

Crown-green bowls foot mat ("footer")

Crown-green bowl, or "wood"

CROWN-GREEN BOWLS *above*
This game is played on a square grass lawn that is raised slightly to form a "crown" in the center. The jack is larger than the one used in the more popular flat-green version.

BOWLING TECHNIQUES *above*
The object of bowls and boules is the same, but boules can be thrown, and bowls must always be rolled along the ground. Each bowl is weighted or "biased" on one side so that it curves gently when it is rolled.

BOWLING SHOES
These have flat soles to avoid damaging the green.

Flat-green wood

Flat-green jack

FLAT-GREEN BOWLS
Traditionally, each set of four bowls, or "woods," was made from a single log of the heavy wood *lignum vitae*. The black or brown bowls are now often made from rubber or composition materials instead.

SIR FRANCIS DRAKE
The English admiral Sir Francis Drake is believed to have been playing a form of bowls at Plymouth when the Spanish invasion fleet, or Armada, was sighted in 1588.

A MEDIEVAL BOWLING GAME
Games in which balls are thrown or rolled along the ground toward a target are among the oldest and most popular of all, dating back to the days of the ancient Egyptians.

MARBLES *below*
Roman children used to play a game like marbles, flicking nuts into an area marked on the floor. There are many different forms of the sport, using balls made from glass or baked clay.

Marbles

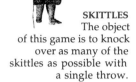

SKITTLES
The object of this game is to knock over as many of the skittles as possible with a single throw.

Most bowlers use a three-finger grip

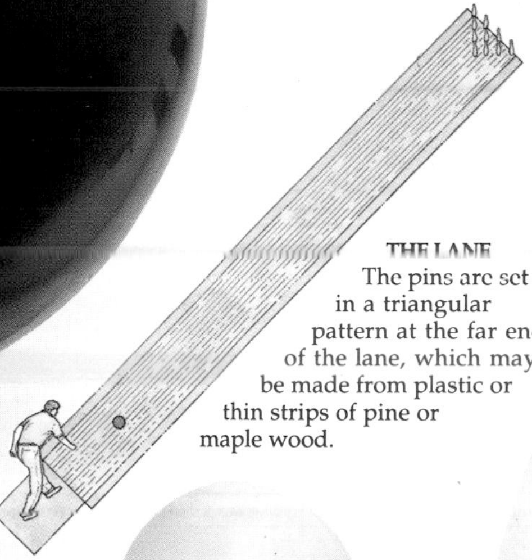

Bowling ball

TENPIN BOWLING
Bowlers roll the heavy ball down a narrow lane, trying to knock down the pins at the other end. Points are scored for each pin knocked down. The ball is made from hard rubber composition or plastic, and may weigh up to 16 lb (7.26 kg). Finger holes are drilled into the ball to make gripping easier.

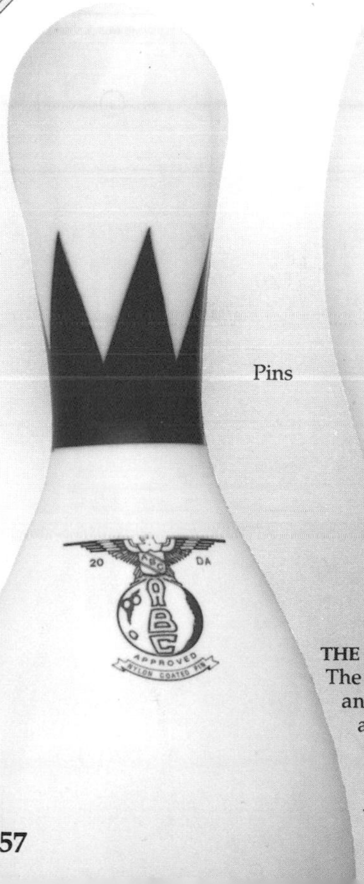

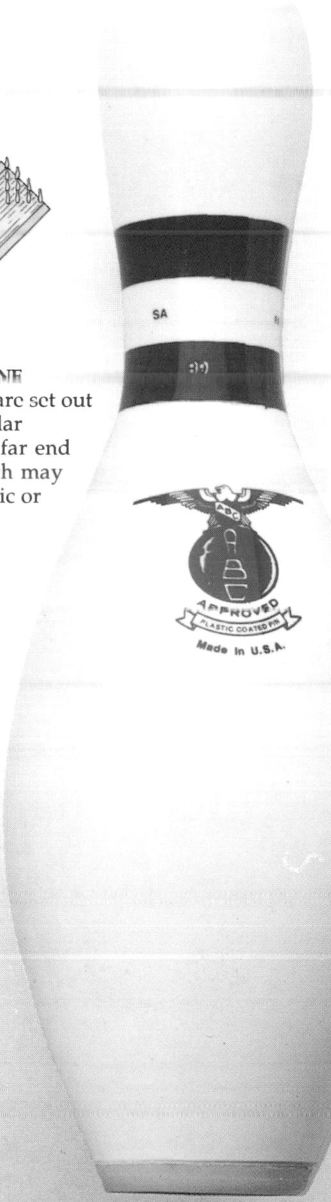

THE LANE
The pins are set out in a triangular pattern at the far end of the lane, which may be made from plastic or thin strips of pine or maple wood.

Pins

CURLING *above*
This is a bowling sport on ice; players slide round "stones" toward a target area called a "house." Brushes are used to sweep away frost and moisture from in front of the running stone. This helps to keep it straight and makes it go farther.

Curling stone

THE PINS
The ten pins are made from maple wood and covered in plastic to protect them against the impact of the ball. Each pin stands on a numbered spot within the formation.

Golf

THE ORIGINS OF GOLF are not clear, but it almost certainly belongs to the same family of sports as bowling and croquet. The modern form of the game was first played in Scotland some 400 years ago. Golfers hit a small ball with clubs from a starting point ("tee") into a hole located some distance away. Modern golf courses have eighteen holes, and the object is to hit the ball into each hole, and so complete the round, using as few strokes as possible.

GOLF CLUBS
A player may use no more than 14 different clubs in any round of golf. Most players use three or four wooden clubs ("woods"), nine or ten metal clubs ("irons"), and a "putter." The ball must be hit with only the head of the club.

WOODS
These clubs have large heads made from wood, or sometimes plastic or metal, and have longer shafts than other clubs. They are capable of hitting the ball a long way and are used for the first tee shot - the "drive" - and for other long shots. The most commonly-used woods are numbered 1 to 5. The number 1 wood, known as the "driver," is the largest.

Number 1 wood

Number 3 wood

Number 5 wood

CLUB HEADS
Wooden clubs are made from persimmon or laminates (layers) of other woods. Face inserts and metal sole plates keep the club from being damaged.

THE SWING *left*
The ball is placed on a small wooden or plastic tee, which raises it off the ground. The golfer takes a great swing at the ball, following through with his club. Hitting the ball straight into the hole from the tee is a "hole in one."

Practice ball

Golf ball

Tee

A TYPICAL HOLE *below*
The length of a hole may be between 300-2000 ft (100-600 m). This length determines its "par" - the number of strokes normally needed to get the ball into the hole. If a player completes a hole in a shot less than par, he scores a "birdie." Two shots less scores an "eagle"; three shots less, a "double eagle". The length and features of each course vary a great deal.

The "tee" is a smooth, level area from which the first shot is taken

Club head ——————

METAL WOODS
Some woods are not wooden at all, but made from metal or plastic.

GOLF BALLS
These are covered with over 400 "dimples," which help the ball fly long and straight when hit. Players use lightweight "air balls" to practice their technique.

Shaft

HEAD COVERS
Special sleeves protect the heads of clubs from the weather when they are not being used.

THE ORIGINS OF GOLF
A stick-and-ball game called "bandy-ball" - a cross between golf and hockey - was played in the 14th century.

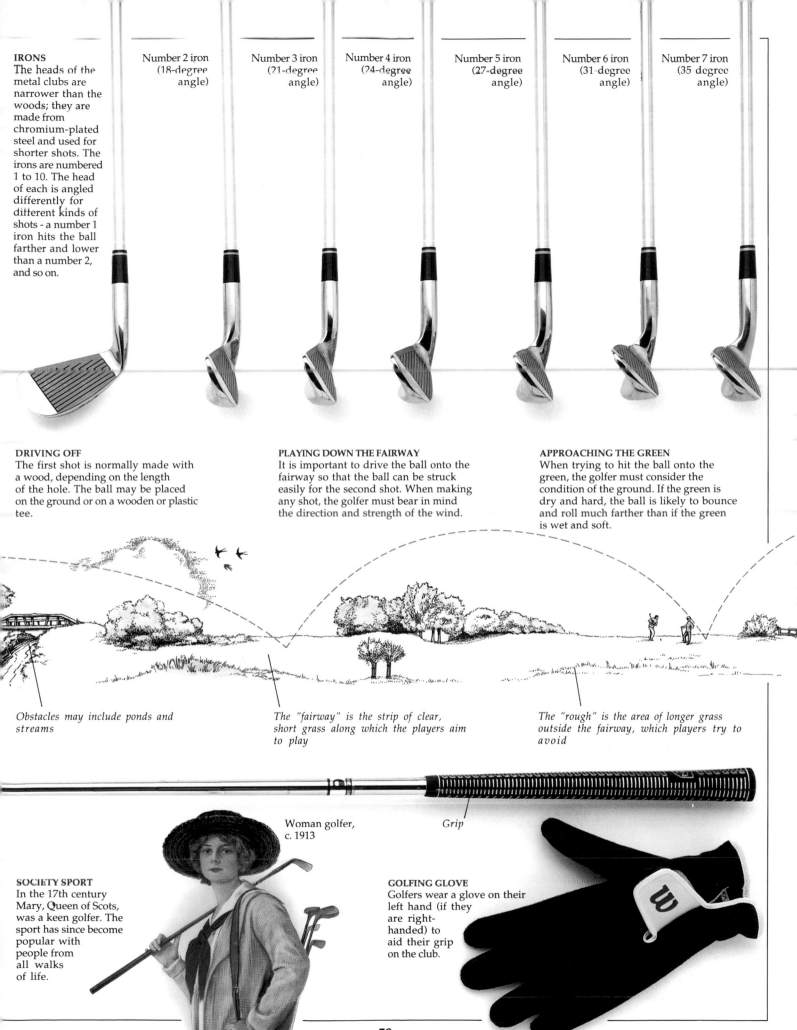

IRONS

The heads of the metal clubs are narrower than the woods; they are made from chromium-plated steel and used for shorter shots. The irons are numbered 1 to 10. The head of each is angled differently for different kinds of shots - a number 1 iron hits the ball farther and lower than a number 2, and so on.

Number 2 iron
(18-degree angle)

Number 3 iron
(21-degree angle)

Number 4 iron
(24-degree angle)

Number 5 iron
(27-degree angle)

Number 6 iron
(31-degree angle)

Number 7 iron
(35-degree angle)

DRIVING OFF
The first shot is normally made with a wood, depending on the length of the hole. The ball may be placed on the ground or on a wooden or plastic tee.

PLAYING DOWN THE FAIRWAY
It is important to drive the ball onto the fairway so that the ball can be struck easily for the second shot. When making any shot, the golfer must bear in mind the direction and strength of the wind.

APPROACHING THE GREEN
When trying to hit the ball onto the green, the golfer must consider the condition of the ground. If the green is dry and hard, the ball is likely to bounce and roll much farther than if the green is wet and soft.

Obstacles may include ponds and streams

The "fairway" is the strip of clear, short grass along which the players aim to play

The "rough" is the area of longer grass outside the fairway, which players try to avoid

Woman golfer, c. 1913

Grip

SOCIETY SPORT
In the 17th century Mary, Queen of Scots, was a keen golfer. The sport has since become popular with people from all walks of life.

GOLFING GLOVE
Golfers wear a glove on their left hand (if they are right-handed) to aid their grip on the club.

Pitching wedge, used to "chip" the ball onto the green (48-degree angle)

Sand wedge, used to get the ball out of a bunker (55-degree angle)

PUTTERS
Putters are light clubs, usually made of metal, and are used only on the putting green. They have flat faces but come in many different designs to suit each player's taste.

Standard center-shaft putter

Large-head putter with angled neck

Small-head center-shaft putter

GETTING OUT OF TROUBLE
If the ball is accidentally hit into a bunker, it can be very difficult to get out. A sand wedge may be used to lift the ball onto the green.

PUTTING
Once the ball is on the green, a putter is used to hit it along the ground and into the hole.

THE PUTTING TECHNIQUE
The ball must be struck with the head of the club - not pushed or "scraped" along the ground. The golfer must take into account the direction of any slope when making his stroke.

Sand traps, or "bunkers," are often placed close to the green

The "green" is the area of very short grass where the hole is located

The hole is marked with a flag known as the "pin"

BALL MARKERS
On the green, players may pick up their ball and mark its position with a small disk while an opponent takes his putt.

GOLF SHOES
Golfers wear shoes with spiked soles to help them stand firm when they are swinging their clubs. The most expensive pair of shoes in the world are mink-lined golf shoes with gold trim and ruby-tipped spikes.

THE CADDIE
The caddie is an assistant who carries the bag of clubs around the course. This is an 18th-century caddie.

60

Croquet

Croquet has much in common with lawn bowls (p. 56), but like golf, the sport involves hitting a ball at a target with a club - or, in this case, a "mallet." A game consists of scoring points by hitting colored balls through a series of arches, or "wickets," in a certain order. The secret of the sport is to keep the balls of your own side close together, and those of the opposing side as far apart as possible. The winner is the player or team that gets all its balls to the end of the course first.

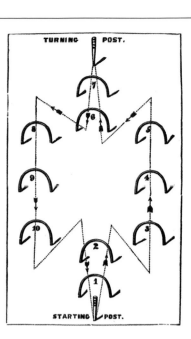

PEGGING OUT
The balls must be hit through each of the six wickets twice, and a point is scored for each wicket. At the end of the course, the player hits the ball against the wooden peg to score an extra point, making a total of 13 for each ball.

A BYGONE AGE
Croquet, like golf, was a fashionable social pastime during the 19th century. The popularity of the sport declined as lawn tennis (p. 30) became all the rage in the late 19th century, but it is now enjoying a revival.

THE TEN-WICKET GAME
Modern croquet matches use just six wickets, but the old-fashioned form of the game used ten. The broad, round-topped wickets used at that time were thought to be much too easy to get the ball through, so they were replaced with the modern narrower kind.

THE CROQUET SHOT
If a player hits his ball into another ball, he is allowed to make a "croquet" shot. He places his ball against the other ball and hits it so that both balls are sent in different directions.

The handle of the mallet is usually made of ash

WICKETS
The iron wickets are just wide enough for the balls to pass through. They are painted white, and the crown of the last wicket, or "rover," is red.

THE BALLS
Each player or team plays with two of the four balls, which are traditionally made from boxwood or composite material.

MALLETS
Players must hit the ball, rather than push it, with the head of the mallet, which is about 32 in (80 cm) long from the tip of the handle to the base of the head.

SINGLES AND DOUBLES
Two players may compete with two balls each, or four players can compete as two teams, with one ball per player. Each player must use the same colored ball throughout the game. Blue and black always play against red and yellow.

The boxwood mallet head may be square or cylindrical

HOCKEY ON HORSEBACK
The sport of polo is like a cross between field hockey (p. 16) and croquet played by teams of four riders on horseback. Long-handled mallets made from sycamore or ash are used to hit a ball toward goals set 900 ft (275 m) apart.

Pool and snooker

THESE INDOOR SPORTS are played on a rectangular table that has "pockets" at the corners and in the middle of the longest sides. Players use long wooden cues to hit balls into the pockets and score points. In the "8-ball" version, each player tries to sink his or her set of balls before the other player sinks his or her set. Both sports evolved from the game of billiards, which dates back to around the 15th century, when it was probably played outdoors on grass. King Louis XI of France is thought to have been the first to play the game indoors.

THE ROYAL MACE
Billiards was popular at the French court at Versailles. Players in Louis XIV's day had to hit the ball with a "mace" - a stick some 3 ft (1 m) long, flattened at one end into a spoon shape.

Over 35 miles (56 km) of woolen yarn are needed to cover a 12ft 6in x 6ft 7in (4 m x 2 m) table

Plain colors

THE TABLE
The first tables were made from oak and marble; the modern slate-bed tables were not introduced until the 1830s. The use of the rigid slate ensures that the playing surface is completely flat. The table is covered with a fine-quality woolen cloth.

8-ball

Striped colors

Slate bed screwed to wooden underframe

POOL BALLS
The pool balls are divided into two groups - numbers 1-7 are called "solids," and numbers 9-15 are called "stripes." In "8-ball" pool each player must pocket all the balls in one of these groups and then sink the black 8-ball to win.

Cue ball

POCKETS
Balls that fall into the holes are collected in string pockets.

Two-piece cues have a screw attachment

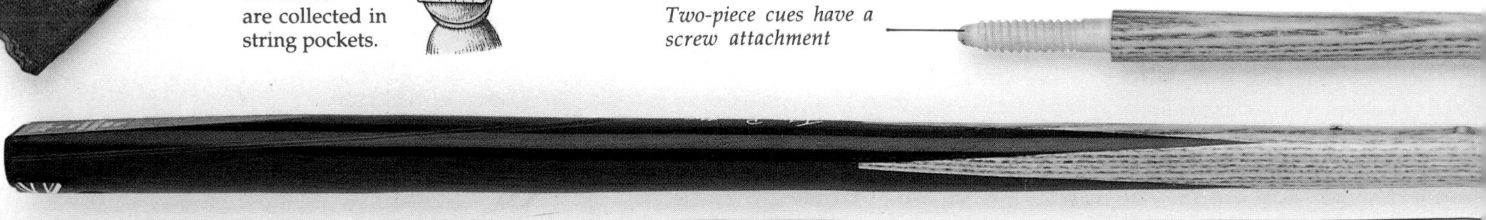

Snooker

The game of snooker was invented by a British Army officer in India in 1875. The term "snooker" was a nickname for military cadets in England at the time. Players score points by sinking the red balls, after which they may attempt a colored ball, which is worth more points. Sunk colored balls are replaced on their spots until no reds are left. The players then try to sink the colored balls in a certain order, finishing with the black ball.

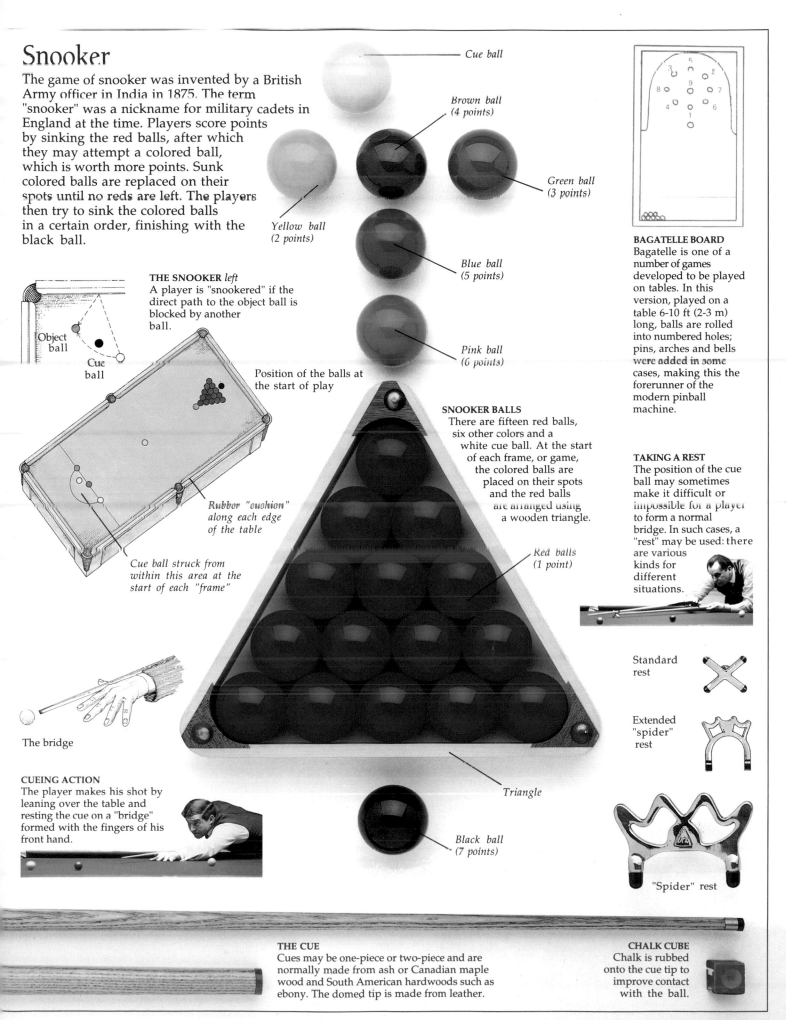

Cue ball

Brown ball
(4 points)

Green ball
(3 points)

Yellow ball
(2 points)

Blue ball
(5 points)

Pink ball
(6 points)

THE SNOOKER *left*
A player is "snookered" if the direct path to the object ball is blocked by another ball.

Object ball

Cue ball

Position of the balls at the start of play

Rubber "cushion" along each edge of the table

Cue ball struck from within this area at the start of each "frame"

The bridge

CUEING ACTION
The player makes his shot by leaning over the table and resting the cue on a "bridge" formed with the fingers of his front hand.

SNOOKER BALLS
There are fifteen red balls, six other colors and a white cue ball. At the start of each frame, or game, the colored balls are placed on their spots and the red balls are arranged using a wooden triangle.

Red balls
(1 point)

Triangle

Black ball
(7 points)

BAGATELLE BOARD
Bagatelle is one of a number of games developed to be played on tables. In this version, played on a table 6-10 ft (2-3 m) long, balls are rolled into numbered holes; pins, arches and bells were added in some cases, making this the forerunner of the modern pinball machine.

TAKING A REST
The position of the cue ball may sometimes make it difficult or impossible for a player to form a normal bridge. In such cases, a "rest" may be used: there are various kinds for different situations.

Standard rest

Extended "spider" rest

"Spider" rest

THE CUE
Cues may be one-piece or two-piece and are normally made from ash or Canadian maple wood and South American hardwoods such as ebony. The domed tip is made from leather.

CHALK CUBE
Chalk is rubbed onto the cue tip to improve contact with the ball.

Did you know?

AMAZING FACTS

In medieval England, townspeople played an early version of soccer against rival towns. Hundreds of people took part and games could last all day long. The matches were incredibly violent; kicking, punching, biting and gouging were permitted. Things got so out of hand that the kings of both England and Scotland tried to suppress soccer. Between 1314 and 1527 no less than nine royal decrees made it an offense to play the game.

Official rugby ball

Researchers who studied England's 1998 World Cup soccer matches found that hospital admissions for heart attacks increased by 25 percent after England lost to Argentina in a nail-biting shoot-out finish.

Today's NFL (National Football League) players earn fantastic salaries, with the average salary topping a cool million dollars. But when the league was founded in 1922 in Canton, Ohio, players considered the low-paying NFL a part-time job, and worked at other jobs during the day. Coaches had to arrange practice sessions in the evenings, when people were off work.

In 1892, the Pittsburgh, Pennsylvania football club, the Allegheny Athletic Association, was locked in a rivalry with the Pittsburgh Athletic Club. The AAA paid former Yale University football star Pudge Heffelfinger 500 dollars to play on their team against the PAC for one crucial game, making Heffelfinger the first professional football player. The money was well spent—Heffelfinger picked up a PAC fumble and ran it for a touchdown.

The first rugby balls were made from pig's bladders, which were inflated using the stem of a clay pipe, before being encased in leather and hand-stitched. Cobbler William Gilbert supplied these bladder balls to the Rugby School in England soon after the first game was played in 1823. His nephew James was in charge of inflating the balls. He blew up the biggest and tightest rugby balls.

The first professional hockey players were a tough crowd—they had to be! In the early days of the game, players wore very little protective gear: just a thick sweater and heavy gloves. Goalkeepers did not wear helmets until 1959, and the National Hockey League did not require helmets until the 1979 season. Today, an average professional hockey goalie wears about 40 pounds (18 kg) of protective gear (mostly tough high-density plastic padding) during a game.

Hockey goalie

When Massachusetts YMCA instructor James Naismith created basketball in 1891, there were just 13 rules, which fit neatly on two typewritten pages. Today, there are an astounding 60 pages in the NBA rulebook.

Traditional topknot hairstyle

A shimekomi, the loincloth worn by a sumo wrestler

Sumo wrestler Konishiki faces a challenger

Silver, gold, and bronze Olympic medals

Olympic athletes must give 100 percent to achieve a gold, silver, or bronze medal. What do they actually get? The gold and silver medals must contain at least 92.5 percent silver, and at least 0.2 ounces (6 grams) of 24-carat gold must coat each gold medal. Bronze medals contain copper, zinc, tin and a very small amount of silver.

On average, 42,000 tennis balls are used and 650 matches are played at the annual Wimbledon tennis tournament held in England.

She routinely drives a golf ball further than 300 yards (274 m), but she's not yet old enough to drive a car. In 2004, Hawaiian golf sensation Michelle Wie became the youngest golfer (and the first female teenager) to play in a PGA tour event. (Tiger Woods made his PGA debut at 16.) Although Wie missed the cut, over the two-day event, she beat or tied 64 men—25 of whom were past winners on the PGA tour.

The longest baseball game with extra innings yet recorded was a 1984 game between the Chicago White Sox and Milwaukee Brewers. The game lasted 25 innings, clocking in at 8 hours and 6 minutes.

The biggest sumo wrestler on record is Samoan-American Seleeva Fuali Atisanoe, known as Konishiki, who retired in 1997. He tipped the scales at an astonishing 589 pounds (267 kg).

BASE jumping from a clifftop

Q What are considered to be the most dangerous sports?

A One strong contender is BASE jumping (Building, Antennae, Span, and Earth are the fixed objects BASE jumpers will leap from—including the Eiffel Tower or the Golden Gate Bridge). Free divers plunge up to 400 ft (122 m) underwater with a single breath; cave divers explore underwater caves more than 100 ft (30 m) deep. Speed skiers wear special skis to reach deadly speeds of 160 mph (257 km/h).

Q How did sports evolve and spread across the globe?

A Sport-like pastimes are common to all times and all places. Most sports developed around the essential skills needed for everyday life, such as hunting (archery), transportation (running, horseback riding, or swimming), or warfare (sword fighting or wrestling). But sports also evolved that had a strong element of play, such as ball games. These included baseball-like games such as the North African *om el mahag* and the Indian *gulli danda*, as well as games resembling modern handball, such as the *tlaxtli* played in Central America. An early form of polo was popular in many Asian countries. But many early sports were closely linked to a specific place. Their rules, the number of players, and the length of the game varied from one place to the next, and there were no regular competitions. In the 1800s, following England's lead, many Western countries set up sports clubs and national sporting organizations, and sports began to evolve globally.

Q What is the oldest ball game in the world?

A The Mesoamerican ball game of *ulama* is probably the world's oldest. Archeologists have found evidence that it was played as far back as 1500 B.C.

Q What is the world's most popular professional sport?

A Soccer is often named the world's most popular sport. Millions of people in more than 140 countries are soccer fans, and the World Cup (held every four years) draws huge global television audiences. European League games are also broadcast to audiences all over the world. A recent survey to determine favorite televised sports put soccer in the lead everywhere but in North America and India.

Q Why is soccer so popular as a participation sport?

A Soccer (called football in most places outside the United States) is one of the most accessible and adaptable sports. In the last 30 years, soccer has become incredibly popular as a participation sport among school-age children in the United States, partly because the rules are relatively simple, and also because the game can be enjoyed by children of all ages and ability levels. The explosion of interest in soccer in America is now making an impact at the professional levels, with men's and women's teams competing globally.

Q Who attends live sporting events around the world?

A A recent survey shows that attending a professional sporting event is more popular in China than anywhere else. Over half of Chinese respondents had attended a sports event in the three months prior to the survey. Worldwide, 23 percent of respondents attended live events. Another study found that more than 80 percent of Americans attend at least one live sporting event a year, and many attend on a regular basis. But the French seem to take their sports most seriously; 78 percent of survey respondents admit to getting into a heated argument over the performance of favorite teams or players.

Record Breakers

MOST KNOCKOUTS IN A PROFESSIONAL BOXING CAREER:
Archie Moore, 129 knockouts

MOST CAREER STRIKEOUTS PITCHED IN BASEBALL:
Nolan Ryan, 5,714 strikeouts

MOST CAREER PROFESSIONAL TENNIS TITLES:
Men: Jimmy Connors, 109
Women: Martina Navratilova, 167

MOST GOALS IN A PROFESSIONAL SOCCER CAREER:
Pelé, 1,279 goals

HIGHEST TOTAL CAREER RUSHING YARDAGE IN FOOTBALL:
Walter Payton, 16,726 yards (15 m)

MOST GOALS IN A PRO HOCKEY CAREER:
Wayne Gretzgy, 894 goals

Fans pack a stadium in Pasadena, California, for the 1999 women's soccer World Cup

Who's who?

YOU'VE LEARNED ALL ABOUT the world of sports—now meet some of the greatest athletes of all time. While it is difficult for sportswriters and fans to agree on a list of top athletes, the people featured here have appeared on many lists of all-time greats. Interestingly, a number of these incredible athletes had two things in common: playing their career sport in childhood and excelling in more than one sport.

Muhammad Ali delivers a punch

MUHAMMAD ALI (1942–)
The world's greatest heavyweight boxer, as well as a hero to many, Muhammad Ali was born Cassius Clay, Jr., in Louisville, Kentucky. After his bicycle was stolen at the age of 12, Clay decided to learn to fight. During high school he racked up boxing wins and in 1960, won a gold medal in the Rome Summer Olympics. Five years later, Clay was crowned heavyweight champion of the world for the first time. In the 1960s, he joined the Nation of Islam faith and changed his name to Muhammad Ali. Legendary title bouts such as the "Rumble in the Jungle" against George Foreman in Zaire in 1974, and the "Thrilla in Manila" against Joe Frazier in 1975 helped confirm Ali's reputation as the "Greatest." His career record when he retired in 1981 was an incredible 56 wins— 37 by knockout—against 5 losses.

NADIA COMANECI (1961–)
Romanian-born athlete Nadia Comaneci was the first gymnast ever to be awarded a perfect score of 10 in an Olympic event. She began winning contests in Romania by the age of nine. At 14, Comaneci was the star of the 1976 Summer Games in Montreal, Canada, winning five medals and racking up one perfect score after another. Comaneci continued to compete until she retired in 1981.

Nadia Comaneci

WAYNE GRETZKY (1961–)
Known as the "Great One," Canadian native Wayne Gretzky is considered by many to be the best ice hockey player of all time. By the age of six, he was playing with 10-year-olds. Just 10 years later, he was on the ice for the Ontario Hockey League. When the National Hockey League was formed in 1979, Gretzky began his record-breaking NHL career. In his first season in the NHL, he was named the league's most valuable player (a feat he repeated the next seven years). During the 1980s, Gretzky continued to smash ice-hockey scoring records. By the time he skated off the ice in his last season of 1998–1999, he held or shared 61 NHL records. His jersey number, 99, was retired by all teams in the league.

SONJA HENIE (1912–1969)
Thought by most to be the greatest female figure skater in history, the Norwegian icon won the first of 10 consecutive World Figure Skating Championships in 1927 at the age of 15. Henie went on to win gold in the 1928, 1932, and 1936 Winter Olympics, as well as winning six consecutive European championships. She was the first skater to wear a short-skirt costume and to use dance choreography, and was also an accomplished tennis player. After the 1936 Olympics she took up a career as a professional performer in movies and live shows.

MIA HAMM (1972–)
Hamm is widely recognized as the world's best all-around women's soccer player. Born in Alabama, she led the University of North Carolina team to four NCAA championships from 1989 to 1993. In 1996 at the Atlanta Centennial Olympic Games, she led the U.S. to team gold in front of 80,000 fans, the most spectators ever to watch a women's sporting event. She also helped the U.S. bring home the 1999 Women's World Cup.

MICHAEL JORDAN (1963–)
Born in Brooklyn, New York, Jordan is known as the best basketball player in history. When he ended his 15-season career, his regular-season scoring average was 30.12 points—the best in NBA history. Jordan won six championships, 10 scoring titles, and was named the league's most valuable player five times. Jordan usually played as a shooting guard, but he was versatile and skilled enough to play point guard or small forward. In 1993 Jordan retired, but he returned to professional sports in 1994 to pursue a baseball career— perhaps following a childhood dream after the sudden death of his father. In 1995, he rejoined the Chicago Bulls, leading the team to three consecutive NBA titles between 1996 and 1998. Jordan retired again in 1999.

Imran Khan

JACKIE JOYNER-KERSEE (1962–)
Winner of three gold, one silver, and one bronze Olympic medals, track-and-field star Joyner-Kersee often tops sportswriter's lists as the best all-around female athlete in the world, bar none. Born in East St. Louis, Illinois, she was inspired to compete in multidiscipline events after seeing a movie about Babe Didrikson (see next page). Joyner-Kersee was the first woman to score 7,000 points in a heptathlon (a seven-event competition) in the 1986 Goodwill Games.

BILLIE JEAN KING (1943–)
One of the greatest tennis players in history, King won the triple crown for singles, doubles, and mixed doubles in both the United States and Britain. The California native is also the only woman to win U.S. titles on all four surfaces on which tennis is played (grass, clay, indoor, and hard). King is also credited with being one of the first female athletes to speak out against inequality in organized sports. In the famous 1973 "Battle of the Sexes," she challenged and defeated Bobby Riggs before one of the largest-ever live audiences for a televised tennis match.

IMRAN KHAN (1952–)
Khan is seen as Pakistan's finest ever all-round cricket player, and among the greatest all-time players in the world. Khan comes from a family of cricketers. He made his Test debut in 1971 when he was just 18 years old. (Test cricket is an elite five-day form of the sport, regarded as the ultimate "test" of playing ability.) During the course of Khan's 88-Test-match career for Pakistan, he scored 3,807 runs and took 362 wickets.

CARL LEWIS (1961–)
Among Carl Lewis's 10 Olympic medals, an astounding nine are gold. The key events for this native of Birmingham, Alabama, included sprints, relay, and long jump. During the 1980s, Lewis scored win after win. In 1996, the 36-year-old Lewis made an Olympic comeback, winning the long jump and becoming only the third Olympian in history to win four consecutive titles in an individual event.

WILLIE MAYS (1931–)
Center fielder Willie Mays is regarded as one of baseball's greats. Hailing from Alabama, where he excelled in sports as a young man, Mays joined the National League in 1951. His habit of greeting his fellow teammates by saying "Say Hey" earned him his lifelong nickname—the "Say Hey Kid." Every aspect of the game came naturally to Mays. He was an excellent hitter, an outstanding defensive fielder, a great base runner and base stealer, and a reliable field presence. He played 150 or more games in 15 of his 21 seasons. Mays retired in 1973, and the San Francisco Giants retired his number, 24.

JOE MONTANA (1956–)
One of the best quarterbacks in the history of the National Football League, Montana led the San Francisco 49ers to four Super Bowls, and became the only player to win three Super Bowl Most Valuable Player awards. The Pennsylvania native joined the NFL in 1979 and played with San Francisco for 12 seasons. In 1993, he was traded to the Kansas City Chiefs, where he played for two seasons until retiring in 1994. Montana was famous for reviving his team's chances late in the game, earning him the nickname, the "Comeback Kid." His career passing total was 40,551 yards (37,000 m).

MARTINA NAVRATILOVA (1956–)
Born in Prague, Navratilova is a fiercely competitive tennis player with a game that many consider second to none. She turned pro in 1973, and in 1975 became a permanent U.S. resident. It was not until 1978 that Navratilova won her first major title at Wimbledon, but from the 1980s onward she was unstoppable, racking up an amazing 58 Grand Slam titles. As of 2005, she is still playing competitively.

Martina Navratilova

Martina returns the ball with a backhand.

JACK NICKLAUS (1940–)
Known as the "Golden Bear," Ohio's Jack Nicklaus was a major player in professional golfing from the 1960s to the late 1990s. With rival Arnold Palmer, he is credited with turning golf into a major spectator sport. Nicklaus began playing professionally in 1962. Unusual in the sport, he is an excellent putter as well as a long hitter. His winning performances in major tournaments are incredible: three Open Championships, four U.S. Opens, six Australian Opens, five PGA (Professional Golfer's Association) championships, and six U.S. Masters. He became the oldest player ever to win the Masters in 1986, and continued to play great golf through his announced retirement in 2005.

JESSE OWENS (1913–1980)
Most famous for his participation in the 1936 Summer Olympics in Berlin, Germany, where he won four gold medals, James Cleveland Owens was an incredible sprinter, long jumper, and hurdler. Owens was born in Alabama and grew up in Cleveland, Ohio. His junior-high-school track coach picked him off the playground and put him on the track team. In a Big Ten meet in 1935, Owens set world records in three events and tied the world record in a fourth event—all in a span of 45 minutes. His stellar performance in the 1936 Olympics was in the record books until 1984, when Carl Lewis won gold medals in the same events.

Pelé

PELÉ (1940–)
Edson Arantes do Nascimento—better known as Pelé—is possibly the finest soccer player of all time. This Brazilian sporting legend was skilled in all areas of the game, from scoring goals, dribbling, and passing, to defensive work on the field. Pelé started his soccer career at 15 with Santos, and he stayed with the team for his entire career. In 1958, he became the world's youngest World Cup winner, and played on two other Cup-winning teams. In 1967, warring factions in Nigeria agreed to a 48-hour cease fire so everyone could watch Pelé play an exhibition game in Lagos. In 1974, he retired from Brazilian soccer and joined the New York Cosmos. He played his last game as a professional in 1977 against his old team, Santos, playing one half for each team.

PETE SAMPRAS (1971–)
Born in Washington, D.C., Pete Sampras found a tennis racket in the basement as a child and spent hours hitting balls against the wall. By the age of 11, he had already developed the serve-and-volley tactic that led him to victory on court. Sampras became the youngest player to win the U.S. Open Men's title, at only 19 years of age. Sampras currently holds the record for the most wins in Grand Slam men's singles events, with a total of 14. He officially retired in 2003.

JIM THORPE (C. 1887–1953)
This incredible athlete won Olympic gold medals, starred in college and professional football, and played major league baseball. Thorpe was a Native American born on a reservation in Oklahoma, later moving to Pennsylvania. Legend has it that he began his athletic career when walking past his school track team. He made an impromptu jump and beat the best jumpers on the team. By 1911, he was a star in college football, scoring a 97-yard (88-meter) touchdown play. In 1913, he played pro baseball with the New York Giants. In 1915, he signed a deal to play pro football with the Canton Bulldogs, one of the first teams in what would later become the NFL. His Olympic medals in track and field events were disputed due to strict rules about professionals participating in the games, but in 1983 they were restored.

TIGER WOODS (1975–)
With his U.S. Amateur win in 1994, Eldrick "Tiger" Woods became the youngest person to ever win that event. Since he became a pro golfer in 1996, the California native has continued his record-breaking career. In 2000, Woods matched Ben Hogan's 1953 record by winning three professional major championships in the same year. When he won the Masters in 2001, he became the only man to have held all four professional golfing majors at once (an achievement nicknamed the "Tiger Slam"). Today, Tiger holds or shares the record for the low score (against par) in each of the four major championships. Like Jack Nicklaus before him, Woods is an excellent driver as well as a superb putter. He is credited with providing a major surge of interest in professional golfing, especially among younger audiences.

BABE DIDRIKSON ZAHARIAS (1911–1956)
An incredible all-around athlete, Mildred "Babe" Didrikson Zaharias won Olympic gold medals for the javelin and 80-meter hurdles, and a silver medal for the high jump. She got her nickname, a reference to Babe Ruth, due to the incredible home runs she routinely knocked out of the park playing baseball as a teenager in Texas. In 1935, Babe took up golf, going on to win 55 professional and amateur events, including three U.S. Opens. She helped found the LPGA (Ladies' Professional Golfing Association) in 1949. When a journalist asked her if there was anything she didn't play, she replied, "Yeah, dolls."

Tiger

Find out more

THIS BOOK HAS INTRODUCED YOU TO THE wide world of sports. Here are some ways you can get your own game on. Whether you are shooting hoops, putting shots, or pitching strikes, participating in sports is rewarding. In addition to providing health and fitness benefits, sports promote self-esteem and social skills, and provide a valuable experience of teamwork. Following a particular sport is a passion shared by millions across the globe. You can catch the excitement by attending a sporting event or watching televised coverage. A visit to one of the sporting halls of fame or a stadium tour will teach you more about the legends and lore of a particular game.

TAKE ME OUT TO THE GAME
Attending a sporting event such as a baseball game can teach you about the ins and outs of a sport, and nothing equals the thrill of being there. Whether you are watching the best athletes in the country or the best on your block, if you put a little effort into how you watch, you may be surprised at how much you can learn.

ROLL WITH IT
If you are interested in a particular sport, why not give it a try? From bowling to baseball, schools and community programs provide plenty of opportunities to participate in organized sports.

SPORTS ON TELEVISION
If you can't be there, you can turn to televised sports. Watching sports (like this Olympic swimming event) on television gives you information that a spectator in the stadium can't get. Running commentary from experts helps you really understand the nuances of the game, and technical innovations such as instant replay and computer graphics let you analyze each play.

USEFUL WEB SITES

www.olympics.org
The official web site of the Olympic movement includes a history of the Olympics, as well as the latest news and an inside guide to the 35 sports currently recognized by the Olympics.

www.mlb.com
The home page of Major League Baseball

www.nba.com
The home of the National Basketball Association

www.nfl.com
The National Football League's official web site

HEY, COACH!

As your playing level improves, you may want to hire a coach for individual lessons. A good coach is a role model and a strong motivator, as well as someone who can help you take your game to its highest level. When you improve your game, you get the satisfaction that comes from mastering a skill. If individual lessons are not affordable, sign up for group lessons.

TAKE A STADIUM TOUR

Maybe you're not ready for the big leagues just yet, but you can experience a taste of what it's like by taking a behind-the-scenes stadium tour. It's a thrill for a sports fan to actually step onto the playing field. Contact the information office of a nearby sports stadium or check the Internet to find out what options are available.

MEETING THE PROS

Make sure to pack a felt-tip pen when you attend a sporting event. You never know when you are going to run into a pro player, and you may get a chance to politely ask for an autograph when you do! Some professional sports teams hold fan-appreciation days, with scheduled autograph signings, prize giveaways, and photo opportunities.

Places to Visit

HOCKEY HALL OF FAME AND MUSEUM, TORONTO, ONTARIO
Visit this shrine to players, coaches, referees, and sportswriters, and see a rich collection of artifacts.

INTERNATIONAL BOXING HALL OF FAME, CANASTOTA, NEW YORK
Boxing's rich history and the tales of its epic championship battles are chronicled here.

INTERNATIONAL TENNIS HALL OF FAME, NEWPORT, RHODE ISLAND
Interactive exhibits, videos, and memorabilia capture the history of the game of tennis.

NAISMITH MEMORIAL BASKETBALL HALL OF FAME, SPRINGFIELD, MASSACHUSETTS
Experience the rich history and hoopla surrounding this classic American game.

NATIONAL BASEBALL HALL OF FAME AND MUSEUM, COOPERSTOWN, NEW YORK
Explore America's pastime through artifacts, photographs, and interactive exhibits.

PRO FOOTBALL HALL OF FAME, CANTON, OHIO
A bronze statue of Jim Thorpe greets guests as they enter this museum dedicated to the history of football as well as each of the NFL teams.

NATIONAL SOCCER HALL OF FAME AND MUSEUM, ONEONTA, NEW YORK
This museum dedicated to the history and heroes of soccer features an interactive Kicks Zone that lets visitors get in on the action.

VISIT A SPORTING HALL OF FAME

A visit to one of the halls of fame dedicated to a particular sport is a must for any true fan. These museums (including the Baseball Hall of Fame, left) honor the most legendary figures in sporting history, and their collections of memorabilia are outstanding. You may be able to schedule a visit to a hall of fame induction ceremony, held once a year. Community festivals, parades, pro games, and a gathering of inductees past and present make these events special.

Glossary

AIR VALVE A device that opens or closes to allow air in or out; for example, to inflate a football or soccer ball

ARTIFICIAL GRASS A carpetlike material developed to replace real grass on sporting fields. It was first developed (under the trademarked name of Astroturf) for use in the Houston Astrodome, after the dome's natural lawn grass deteriorated.

BLADDER A bag that fills with air; for example, inside a soccer ball

BUNKER On a golf course, a hazard consisting of a prepared area of ground (often a hollow) from which the soil has been removed and replaced with sand. A bunker also describes a natural depression on a fairway or around the green.

CADDIE A person who carries or handles a golf player's clubs, and who may advise the player on the course of the game

CLAY PIGEON A target used in skeet or trapshooting

Clay pigeon

CLEAN AND JERK A type of weightlifting in which the barbell is lifted up to shoulder height and then jerked overhead

CROSSBOW A shooting device, in which a bow is placed crosswise on a stock. Crossbows fire bolts, which are much shorter than regular archery arrows.

CUE A tapering wooden rod used to strike the cue ball in the game of pool or billiards

CURLING A game played on ice in which curling stones (heavy stones with handles) are slid toward a target

DECATHALON In the Olympic Games, a two-day contest of ten events

DIAMOND The diamond-shaped area of a baseball field that is enclosed by three bases and home plate

DISCUS An athletic competition in which a disc-shaped object is thrown as far as possible. The object itself is also a discus.

ÉPÉE A light dueling sword in the sport of fencing, with a large bell guard and a blade with a triangular cross-section

FACE-OFF In hockey, when the referee drops the puck between two opposing players in order to start or resume the game

FAIRWAY In golf, the playing area of cut grass located between the tee and the green

FENCING The sport of fighting with special swords, with points scored according to an official set of rules

FLETCHING The name for the feathers attached to an arrow that help to stabilize it during flight

FOIL In fencing, a light, slender, flexible sword tipped with a button

GAUNTLET Used in many sports, a padded glove with a long sleeve, used to protect the hand and wrist

GOAL The piece of equipment or playing-field area toward which players of a game try to advance a ball or puck, for example, in order to score points

Crossbow

GOAL LINE In football, the line at each end of the playing field 10 yards (9 m) from the end line, and over which the ball must be carried or passed to score a touchdown

GOALKEEPER In many sports, the player positioned directly in front of the goal who tries to prevent shots from getting into the net behind him

GOALPOST A tall structure at the back of each end zone in football, consisting of a crossbar and two uprights that extend upward from it, supported by a base. Teams try to kick the ball above the crossbar and between the uprights to score a field goal or make an extra point.

GREEN An area of closely cropped grass surrounding the hole on a golf course

GRIDIRON A football field

HAMMER An athletic competition in which a heavy metal ball that is attached to a flexible wire is hurled as far as possible

HEADING In soccer, directing and moving the ball by striking it with your head

A pair of fencers in a duel

HEPTATHLON A seven-event women's contest in the Olympic Games, created in 1984, consisting of the shot put, 100-meter hurdles, javelin, high jump, long jump, 200-meter dash, and 800-meter run.

HOLE IN ONE In golf, when the ball goes straight into the hole from the player's tee shot; also called an ace

HOME RUN In baseball, a base hit where the batter is able to touch all three bases and return to home before being put out

JAVELIN An athletic competition in which a javelin (a spearlike weapon) is thrown as far as possible

KICKING TEE A support that holds a football on one end, slightly above ground, in preparation for the kickoff

KNOCKOUT In boxing, a blow that renders the opponent unconscious

LACROSSE A game in which two teams attempt to send a ball into each other's goal, each player using a crosse (or stick) topped with a netted pocket for catching, carrying, or throwing the ball

LINESMAN An official who assists the referee. A linesman must indicate when a ball (or puck) is out of play or offsides.

LOB In tennis, a stroke in which the ball is hit in a high arc, usually used to get the ball over an opponent at the net

LONG BOW In archery, a bow drawn by hand in contrast to a crossbow

MALLET A sports implement with a long handle and a head like a hammer, used in sport such as polo or croquet to hit a ball

Nunchaku

NUNCHAKU In martial arts, a weapon consisting of two wooden handles joined by a metal chain

OLYMPIC GAMES The modern revival of the ancient Greek games, with staggered summer and winter games held once every four years in selected countries

PENALTY Punishment of a player or team official for violation of the rules, often resulting in the removal of the player or official for a specific period of time

PITCH In baseball, the throwing of the ball by a pitcher to a batter; in golf, a high-approach shot

POLE VAULT An athletic competition that involves jumping over a high crossbar with the aid of a long pole

POMMEL HORSE A device used in gymnastics consisting of a cylindrical body covered in leather, with two upright handles (pommels) near the center

PUCK A black, vulcanized rubber disk used to play hockey. The puck can travel up to 120 mph (193 km/h) on a slap hot.

PUTT In golf, the rolling shot taken on the green, with a club called a putter

Gymnast on a pommel horse

QUARTERBACK In football, the backfield player who receives the ball from the center on most offensive plays. The quarterback calls signals, throws forward passes, and may sometimes run with the ball down the field.

QUIVER In archery, a case designed for holding arrows

RACKET A sports implement usually consisting of a handle and an oval frame with a tightly interlaced network of strings, used to strike a ball (or shuttlecock) in various sports

REAL TENNIS An ancient form of tennis played in a four-walled court; also called royal tennis;

REFEREE The official who supervises the game, calls penalties, and determines if points are scored. The referee has the final decision over all other officials.

REST A support on which a piece of equipment, such as a pool cue, can be rested

RING A square platform, marked off by ropes, in which athletes box or wrestle

RINK The name for the iced area inside the boards on which the game of hockey is played. It is rectangular with round corners.

ROUGH The part of a golf course near the fairway, where the grass is not cut short

SABER A fencing sword with a V-shaped blade and a slightly curved handle

SCRUM The method of beginning play in rugby, in which the forwards of each team crouch side by side with locked arms. Play begins when the ball is thrown in between them and the two sides compete for possession.

SERVE In sports, any stroke that puts the ball into play

SHOT In sports, the act of swinging or striking at a ball with a club, racket, bat, cue, or hand; also, in athletics, the heavy metal ball used in the shot put event

SHUTTLECOCK In badminton, the object used instead of a ball, consisting of a rounded piece of cork or rubber with a crown of feathers

SOFTBALL A game resembling baseball played on a smaller diamond, with a ball that is larger and softer. This is also the name for the ball itself.

STARTING BLOCK A device attached to the track, providing firm bracing for a runner's feet at the start of a race

STRIKE ZONE In baseball, the area over home plate between the batter's armpits and knees when the batter is in position to swing. A pitch delivered through this area is called a strike.

STUMP In cricket, any of the three upright wooden posts that form the wicket

SYNTHETIC Refers to something that is produced artificially

TARGET In shooting or archery, the object set up for a marksman or archer to take aim at

TEE In golf, the starting place for each hole on the course; also, the short peg that is put in the ground to hold the golf ball up off the grass during a player's swing

UMPIRE An official or other referee in a sports competition

VOLLEY A tennis return made by hitting the ball before it bounces

VOLLEYBALL A game in which two teams hit an inflated ball over a high net using their hands; also the name for the ball itself

Rugby teams in a scrum

WICKET In cricket, a set of three stumps topped by crosspieces, at which the ball is bowled; a wicket is also a count of the number of outs in an inning

WICKETKEEPER In cricket, the fielder who stands immediately behind the striker's wicket

WIMBLEDON The annual international tennis championships played annually in Wimbledon, a suburb of London, England

WORLD CUP A soccer tournament held every four years between national soccer teams to determine a world champion

Index

Acknowledgments

The publisher would like to thank:
Grandstand Sports and Leisure
Geron Way
Edgware Road
London NW2

A & D Billiards & Pl Services Ltd, Amateur Athletics Association, Amateur Boxing Association, Amateur Fencing Association, Badminton Association of England Ltd, Bapty and Co. Ltd, Billiards and Snooker Control Council, British Amateur Baseball and Softball Federation, British Amateur Gymnastics Association, British Amateur Weight Lifters' Association, British American Football Association British Ice Hockey Federation, British Racketball Association, British Tenpin Bowling Association, Jonathan Buckley, Continental Sports Products Co., The Croquet Association, Dragon Marial Arts, English Basketball Association, English Bowling Association, English Table Tennis Association, The Football Association, The Football League

Ltd, C.L. Gaul & Co. Ltd, James Gilbert Ltd, Grand national Archery Society, Grays of Cambridge (International) Ltd, Gridiron Sports, International Hockey Federation, Quicks the Archery Specialist, Leon Paul Equipment Co. Ltd, Charlie Magri Sports, Martial Arts Commission, Marylebone Cricket Club, Minerva Footbal co. Ltd, Diana Morgan, Newitt & Co. Ltd, Professional Golfers Association, The Rugby Football Union, Len Smiths (School & Sports) Ltd, Squash Rackets Association, Wilson Sporting Goods Co. Ltd, Wimbledon Lawn Tennis Museum.

Ray Owen for artwork

Polyflex running-track materials (pp. 3 and 39) used by courtesy of Recreational Surfaces Ltd

Picture credits
t=top b=bottom m=middle l=left r=right
All-sport (UK): 6tr, bm; 7m; 9b; 10t, mr; 11tr; 13tm, ml; 14br; 16ml; 18tr; 19tm, br; 20tl, bl; 21bl; 23bm;

26mr; 27m; 35ml, bl, 36bl; 37ml; 38tl, bl; 39tl, m; 40tr, br; 47tl; 48 bl, mr; 50bl; 52br; 55tl; 61b; 63mr, bl.
BBC Hulton Picture Library: 10br; 13br; 18tl; 22tr, bl; 25bl; 28ml; 38ml; 40bl; 44tm; 50tl; 51tr, m; 52bl; 53m; 4tl; 55tr; 57tl, tr; 62tr.
The British Library: 54br.
The British Museum: 49tm.
Colorsport/SIPA: 7tm, tr; 9m; 14tr; 15tl; 24bl; 27tl; 31tr, ml; 34m; 42tr, bl; 43bl; 44ml, bm, br45 bl, bm;l 49m; 54m; 58ml.
The Mansell Collection: 34bm; 35br; 56br; 58br.
Mary Evans Picture Library: 8t; 14tl, ml; 15mr; 16tr, bl; 17mr; 25tl, br; 26tl, m; 30br; 31tl; 32tl; 34tl; 37br; 39bl; 41ml, bm; 46bm; 52tl, tr, mr; 57bl; 59bl; 60bl; 61ml.

Cigarette and card illustrations on pp. 42-43 reproduced courtesy of W.D. & H.O. Wills

Illustrations by Will Giles: 10m, bl; 30ml; 35tl; 38mr; 40tr; 57m; 62bl; 63ml.

Illustrations by Sandra Pond: 6m; 13tr, m; 16mr; 19tl; 20mr; 21tl; 22bl; 24mr; 26tr; 39m; 40b; 46ml, m; 51m.

Illustration by Coral Mula: 58-60m.

AP Wideworld: 64tr, 66tl
Corbis: Tony Arruza 68tl; Bettmann 66bl; Jerry Cooke 67tc; Duomo 65bl, 69cl; Ales Fevzer 66tr; Patrik Giardino 67bl; Dimitri Iundt 64bl; London Aerial Photo Library 69tr; Tony Roberts 67br; David Stoecklein 64cr
Getty Images: 66tr, 67cl; Stone 69tl
Orad Hi-Tec Systems Ltd.: 68cl
Picture Quest: Thomas Ulrich 65tr

Jacket images: *Front:* Getty Images: Allsport Concepts (c).

Picture research by:
Joanne King

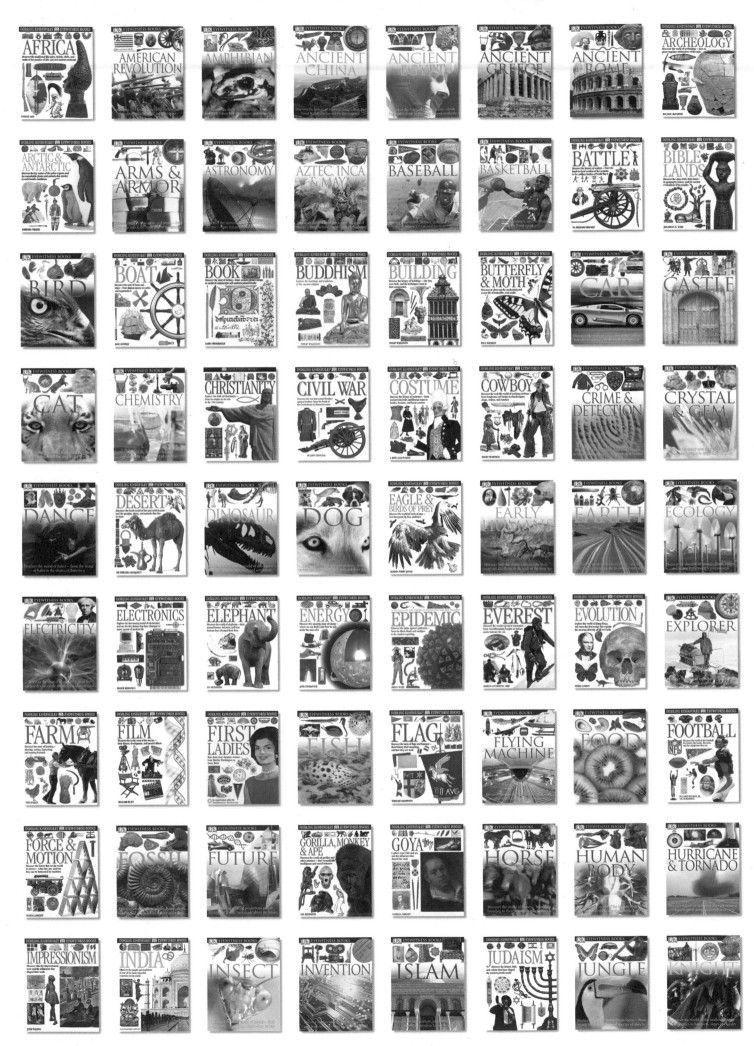